N
River
Guide

Paddling and Fishing in North Carolina, Virginia, and West Virginia

SECANT
PUBLISHING

Bruce Ingram

Includes Coverage of the South Fork and Updated How-To Tips and Access Info

To my best friend and wife, Elaine,
who proofread the entire book
and who is a wonderful wife, mother,
and schoolteacher.

Also to my daughter Sarah and my son Mark—
in your lifetime, may you come to love the outdoors
like I do.

1 Confluence
2 Mouth of Wilson
3 Bridle Creek
4 Independence
5 Baywood
6 Riverside
7 Oldtown
8 Fries
9 Byllesby Dam
10 Buck Dam (Fowler's Ferry)
11 Austinville
12 Jackson Ferry (Foster Falls)
13 Claytor Lake Dam
14 Bissett Park
15 Peppers Ferry Bridge
16 Whitethorne
17 McCoy Falls (Big Falls)
18 Eggleston
19 Pembroke
20 Ripplemead
21 Bluff City
22 Rich Creek
23 Glen Lyn
24 Shanklins Ferry
25 Bluestone Dam
26 Brooks Falls
27 Sandstone Falls
28 Glade Creek
29 McCreery
30 Thurmond

Interstate Highway
274 State Highway
58 US Highway
Campground
Boat Landing
I II III IV Rapids, class
AP Access point
Fishing spot
Reference point
Trip start

West Virginia
Virginia

Virginia
North Carolina

N
W   E
S

0   3   6   9   12
Scale of Miles

Contents

Introduction

One of the great blessings of my life is to have been born and reared between the James and New Rivers in southwest Virginia. I have lived my entire life in the cradle they form. The two streams have always spoken to my sporting soul, so much so that I wrote a book on the former, the *James River Guide,* and have now penned one on the latter.

Although the two waterways are very close to each other in proximity (less than a ninety-minute drive in places) the James and New are extremely different in personality. Whereas the James for the most part flows through forests, fields, and rural surroundings, the New courses through small hamlets and towns as well as isolated forests and spectacular mountain gorges. The James meanders at a moderate pace throughout the majority of its length with just enough Class I and II rapids sprinkled along the way to keep matters interesting. The New, however, does virtually nothing in moderation. Throughout North Carolina, Virginia, and West Virginia, strong Class II and III rapids punctuate the streambed, and in places, specifically in the Mountain State, Class IV+ rapids are the norm. And just about everywhere one goes on the New, a considerable undercurrent exists as the water of the New always seems to be in a hurry to join with the Gauley, which forms the Kanawha, and then on to the Ohio and Mississippi.

Although both rivers are nationally known among those who enjoy the outdoors, the New deservedly has the greater renown. Canoeists and anglers primarily visit the James, whereas the New attracts those two categories of out-doorsmen as well as rafters, kayakers, rock climbers, bird watchers, and a host of other outdoor enthusiasts from across the country. Also, the New often has two statements repeatedly made about it. The first is that it is the second oldest river in the world next to the Nile, and the second is that the New is one of the few rivers that flow north. Actually, both statements are usually made by those who do not know much about the area. Yes, the New is incredibly old and has been reputed to be anywhere from ten million to three hundred and sixty million years of age. But is only the Nile older, who really knows? As far as being one of the few streams that travels northward, the New is not the only river in the area that flows north. The South and North Forks of the Shenandoah, in Virginia, are rivers fairly close to the New that run northward, but few people make statements about the rarity of their directional paths.

For ease of reference, I have divided this book into four sections. Fly and spin fishermen as well as canoeists, rafters, and bird watchers will hopefully find Section 1 filled with enough how-to tips to make their time spent on the New more enjoyable. The three where-to sections of the New follow:

Section Two: The New River above Claytor Lake

Section Three: The New River below Claytor Lake Dam to Bluestone Lake

Section Four: The New River below Bluestone Lake Dam to Fayette Station

River runners will find these divisions useful if they plan to make extended excursions down the waterway.

Readers should realize that the New, more than many rivers, is a highly changeable waterway. I like to say that the James is comparable to the steady girlfriend who a guy can always count on to be by his side. The New is more like the fickle temptress who is a bit of a shrew and always changes her mind. The information I have presented is the most up to date at the time of publication, but the New's inconstant state, as well as floods and other natural phenomenon can increase or decrease the strength of a rapid as well as alter landmarks. Access points also sometimes change over the course of time. Be sure to check with the outfitters mentioned in the appendix before planning a trip.

I relish my time fishing, canoeing, rafting, and bird watching on the New River. I hope you will come to love this river as I do.

—Bruce Ingram

Recreation Opportunities

Classic Warm Water River Smallmouth Patterns

Whenever I receive accounts of river anglers catching dozens of smallmouths on a day trip, I have to groan. For invariably, those same reports conclude that the fish were mostly "dinks" and that the particular river visited is overpopulated with undersized smallies. I live in Southwest Virginia, and my home is less than an hour's drive from the James River to the north and the New River to the south, two of the finest smallmouth streams in the country. A group of four or five friends and I regularly journey to this duo, and we never catch dozens of fish. Our goal is simple: one keeper "bite" (a strike from a fish fourteen inches or better) per person per hour. All of us annually catch smallmouths in the four-pound plus range, which are trophies anywhere in the country for river bronze-backs. The key to this approach is recognizing the few areas in a stream that actually harbor good-sized fish and then employing the proper lures. Here, then, are six patterns that produce "bites" from spring through fall.

The Deep-Water Ledge and Soft Plastics Pattern/Weighted Streamer

One of my favorite spots on the James River is a massive deep-water ledge that extends some ninety yards in length and some thirty yards in width. This bass sanctuary is well away from both banks. Although it lies in the middle of one of the most heavily fished sections overall of the James, I have never seen anyone work it.

Therein lies part of the appeal of deep-water ledges. They are often far away from the shoreline, and their deep water (this particular ledge features depths of six to fourteen feet) discourages the average fisherman from even considering a cast. Ledges are also home to numerous prey species of smallmouths; crayfish especially dwell in the crevices and rubble that exist in the bowels of this structure. The crawfish factor makes soft plastic imitations of 'dads a superlative bait for ledges. I like to rig my craws with ⅜-ounce bullet sinkers. This better enables them to descend into the depths and to stay there, thus overcoming the pull of a river's current.

On one trip down the James, I used crayfish baits to probe the aforementioned ledge for about thirty minutes as my canoe drifted lazily along. Although I caught several nice fish, I knew the ledge held higher quality bass. To give the fish a different look, I switched to a six-inch plastic worm and worked the area again. I caught a two-pounder and missed another fish of that size. Plastic lizards and Carolina-rigged grubs are other baits that can be used after you first check out the ledge/crawfish pattern. Fly fisherman can employ weighted streamers, nymphs, and crayfish

The Eddy and Crankbait/Spinnerbait/Clouser Minnow Pattern

By definition, an eddy is an area where the "current runs contrary to the main current," or reverses back upon itself like a whirlpool. Because of an eddy's nature, minnows especially become trapped inside as do a number of other forage species. Eddies are favorite hunting grounds of smallmouths and any mossyback found within will be actively engaged in tracking down prey. As such, eddies are ideal places to cast lures such as crankbaits and spinnerbaits, and flies such as Clouser streamers which can be rapidly retrieved.

During a late spring cold front last year, a friend and I failed to find fish at most of our favorite places. The only areas that did generate action were eddies, and interestingly, the mossybacks eagerly whacked crankbaits as if the conditions were entirely favorable. I scored by erratically retrieving Storm Wiggle Warts across rocks; most strikes occurred when the bait glanced off this form of cover. Sometimes in eddies, spinnerbaits will out-produce crankbaits.

Inside tip: Tie on the same ½- to 1-ounce tandem willowleaf spinnerbaits that you do for lake largemouths. These larger blade baits will work better in the heavy current of eddies and attract larger fish, as well.

The Current Break and Grub Pattern

I know a West Virginian who fishes nothing but the current break/grub pattern from spring through fall. He totes along a brown paper bag filled with three-inch motor oil grubs and ¼- to ⅜-ounce jigheads. His best Mountain State smallie topped six pounds and goodness knows how many four- and five-pounders he has derricked aboard. I don't restrict myself just to grubs in motor oil but I do recognize the bass-holding potential of current breaks. Current breaks come in several forms, but the best example is a midstream boulder that is partially submerged. Over time, the force of the water tends to hollow out the water behind a boulder giving smallmouths the greater water depth that they so crave. Those same depressions and the rocks also provide bass with ambush points from which they can lash out at minnows, hellgrammites, and other creatures that drift by. Indeed, these creatures themselves often seek out the slack water behind boulders and end up being consumed there.

Laydown logs are another excellent example of current breaks. Often trees, such as sycamores and silver maples, tumble into a river after the current has washed away a section of the bank. Once these trees come to rest on the bottom, they provide superlative cover and, just like midstream boulders, a refuge for bronzebacks looking to escape the main force of the current. The rubble from old dams and the supports of bridges are other examples of current breaks. On the James, one of my favorite current breaks is a partially submerged station wagon that was washed into the river during a flood several years ago. Current breaks can take many forms and they all can conceal overgrown bronzebacks.

The Grass Bed and Buzzbait Pattern

Back in the 1990s, I was fishing the upper Potomac with Ken Penrod who operates Life Outdoors Unlimited in Beltsville, Maryland. The time was mid-July and although Penrod and I had done well early in the day, the fishing had slowed considerably. To my surprise, the guide maneuvered his jet boat to within casting distance of a grass bed and then began flinging a buzzbait to the edges of the grass. I considered the first two-pounder that Ken caught a fluke, and I became only mildly interested when a second fish lunged at the bait. When another two-pounder crushed this blade bait, I begged Ken for his buzzbait and today that same lure has an honored place in my tackle box. "Ken's Buzzer," as I call it, has produced dozens of jumbo smallies, as have a series of other buzzbaits that I now own. I am not going to attempt to analyze why river smallmouths become so riled when they see a buzzbait churning by them. But I do know that no other bait will entice fish lurking around vegetation like this one does. If you want to maximize the grass bed/buzzbait pattern, learn to recognize the areas where bass are most likely to hold along this cover.

For example, the ideal situation is one where the downstream side of a bed has a drop-off that is at least a foot deeper than any of the water depths at the sides or the upstream side of the vegetation. Smallmouths will lie in this drop-off when they are inactive, but will move up to the edge of the grass when they are ready to feed. And one of the surest bets in river fishing is that an active grass bed bass will crunch a buzzer.

Another super situation is an isolated patch of grass with deep water on at least one of its sides. This type of condition usually occurs when spring floods have washed away part of a small island where vegetation once thrived. Finally, any time the main channel of a river winds its way close to a grass bed, consider

The New River offers outstanding warm water smallmouth sport.

a buzzbait. The grass bed/buzzbait pattern will yield smallmouths throughout the day from late spring through early fall.

I also want to add one tidbit about buzzbaits. Many anglers swear that the color of a buzzbait makes a difference. I disagree. The buzzbait is a pure reaction lure, the color could be pink with orange stipes and it would not matter to the fish.

The Jig and Pig Pattern Fished Deep or Shallow:
An All-Season, All-Purpose Big River Bass Pattern

The best river smallmouth anglers I know all heavily rely on the jig and pig throughout the year. For example, one summer during an excursion down the James, a friend caught and released twenty-two keepers on this bait. His game plan was to cast a ⅛-ounce homemade hair jig tipped with a tiny plastic crayfish trailer to current breaks. On a trip one fall, two of my friends used a ¼-ounce jig and Zoom Salt Chunk to catch a number of fine smallies in the two-pound range. They targeted shoreline cuts with laydown logs. One winter, I entered a river smallmouth tournament and, you guessed it, anglers using jigs with pork trailers produced all the top catches. The preceding year, my best spring small-mouth, a four-pounder, fell to a ½-ounce jig with a pork trailer. That smallmouth came from a submerged logjam in an eddy. In short, you can employ the jig and pig as the main lure for any of the hot spots in the aforementioned patterns. Some anglers prefer hair jigs, while others opt for homemade versions made from a variety of compounds. Still others like the synthetic models on the market today. Some anglers select soft plastic trailers, while others go for the traditional pig. No matter, the jig and pig is a necessary bait for the serious river angler. This book won't help you catch a hundred fish per day, as so many river anglers like to do. But the patterns mentioned can lead to you catching more high-quality brown bass.

The Damsel and Dragonflies Pattern of Blane Chocklett: Great for Warm Water

During the warm water season, two of the favorite foods of stream small-mouths are also two of the hardest patterns for fly fishermen to create: the damsel and dragonflies. For years, guide Blane Chocklett was frustrated by this fact.

"I didn't like any of the damsel or dragonfly imitations on the market," he recalls. "Some of them didn't float well, some weren't durable, and some didn't look like the real things. So one day, I was sitting at my bench and braiding some material, and I thought that if I could use this material to create the body of a damsel fly, it would look really nice."

After the concept occurred to him, Chocklett says it was simple to flesh out the wings and the rest of the fly. Indeed, with their shimmering blues, greens, and yellows, the Roanoker's creations are quite striking—the most true-to-life Odonata imitations that this writer has seen. Chocklett suggests that long rodders cast his damsel and dragonflies to water willow beds, undercut banks, and at the head and tail ends of pools. Interestingly, Chocklett says his flies have a bass-bewitching, undulating motion when they are slowly twitched, a trait that makes them good choices for riffles.

Some four hundred damsel and dragonfly species exist in North America, and scores thrive along rivers. Blane Chocklett can't fashion patterns to match all those species, but he has made a fine start on duplicating the appearance of several that live in the Southeast.

Falling for the New's Autumn Smallmouths

Positioning our boat within casting distance of a series of laydowns in six to eight feet of water, my buddy and I began working ½-ounce jig and pigs around the wood. On my fifth cast to the heavy cover, I received a strike and I used a medium-heavy baitcaster (spooled with 14-pound-test line) to derrick the four-pound bass from the cover.

Scenes like this occur every autumn across America on the country's best largemouth lakes as the fish become more active after experiencing the summer doldrums. My friend and I weren't on an impoundment, however. We were in a canoe and fishing for river smallmouths. The typical river smallmouth story line details how an angler "employs small baits, light line, and light action rods for these feisty little fighters that inhabit the swift moving, shallow sections of streams." If you are interested in catching dozens of eight- to ten-inch smallies, then this approach is quite sound. But if you want larger river bronzebacks this autumn, you need to fish like impoundment fishermen do when they go after bigger bass. Fish the same locations with the same types of lures that they use.

Where to Find the Big Ones

Certain types of lairs attract overgrown river smallmouths throughout the fall. One of my favorite places is the tail end of a pool below a rapid. During the summer, smallies are more likely to hold where the rapid first breaks into the pool. But by the fall, as the water temperature decreases, the fish tend to go farther away from the swift water and set up.

Another likely locale is a relatively deep pool along a shaded outside bend. Even with the water temperature lower now, smallmouths still seem to retain their penchant to ambush prey from shaded lairs. Bass tend to avoid full sun areas except during the winter and early spring.

Several other big smallmouth honey holes are also worth mentioning. One is a series of deep-water ledges that rest in water at least six feet deep. Sometimes, the top of the ledge may even be visible above the surface. This type of spot is such a sweet one in the fall because of the deep water between these ledges. Numerous prey species (crayfish, minnows, sculpins, mad toms, and various aquatic insects) frequent the nooks and crannies of these ledges and overgrown smallmouths do, as well.

Another marvelous location is a bank with numerous cuts or indentations along its shoreline; that is, if those cuts contain underwater logs and water five or more feet deep. Many river fishermen don't associate wood with smallmouths, and they are correct to the point that few smallies actually hold around wood. But a log in deep water will often harbor a two-, three-, or even a four-pound mossyback and such cover is well worth checking out. During the fall, a deep-water laydown pattern will produce throughout the day. Focus on logs that are at least partially in the shade. Generously endowed mossybacks wait there in ambush.

Another consistent locale is a deep-water pool. Barry Loupe, another outstanding fisherman, maintains that a deep pool with a rapid at its head can attract large smallies, especially in early to mid-fall. Look for the smallmouths to periodically move into eddies on the sides of that pool where they will dine on creatures that have been washed into and trapped in the reversing currents there. Indeed, both Loupe and I agree, the only time to fish thin water for good-sized river smallmouths is very early on a warm autumn day when the nicer fish have temporarily moved shallow before the sun rises.

How to Catch the Big Ones

One of my favorite fall baits is a little bit of a surprise, a Rebel Pop-R. As long as the water temperature falls no lower than the upper 50s, a topwater bite will exist. It won't be as predictable or as long as the one that occurs from late spring through summer, but it will happen. I am more likely to let the popper drift along than give it violent jerks.

Another great choice is a soft plastic jerkbait. I prefer the four-inch size because it is the size of large minnows and small chubs this time of year. Let the jerkbait fall slowly to the bottom and give it a gentle twitch every now and then.

Barry Loupe says that his preferred bait on the New River and the North Fork of the Holston where he lives is a lake angler's favorite: the venerable jig and pig. Loupe belongs to a river fishing bass club that holds tournaments on the North Fork. In a recent year, some 90 percent of the anglers who won the big smallmouth prize for those events were fishing a jig and pig. "Another terrific artificial," continues the guide, "is a six-inch finesse worm." Loupe and his frequent fishing partner, Johnny Cregger of Saltville, together caught twelve smallmouths of twenty inches or longer on this bait during a recent six-month period. And the guide says he has no idea how many two- and three-pound smallies fell for this bait. The Virginian rigs this straight-tail worm with a split-shot and tosses it to deep water runs in the mid-river area. Then he merely lets the worm drift along with the current in a very natural manner.

Like lake largemouth fishermen and like Loupe, I rely a great deal on soft plastic baits for jumbo bass. Two of my *go-to* lures are Mister Twister or Zoom six-inch curl tail worms and four-inch craw worms, rigged Texas-style. A crucial part of fishing these baits is to use at least ⅜-ounce bullet sinkers with them. On several trips, the heavier weight has made a difference.

For example, I recently took float trips on Virginia's James River and West Virginia's South Branch of the Potomac. On both excursions, my best fish were fat three-pounders that fell to a heavily weighted plastic worm. The jumbo James fish was holding in ten feet of water between two large boulders where the current rumbled through. The South Branch bronzeback was lurking at the end of a rocky shoreline in eight feet of water where the main channel swung in close to the bank. If I had been tossing small soft plastic bait with a ⅛-ounce weight, I doubt that these larger fish would have been interested in my offering. Indeed, they wouldn't have seen it at all before the current unceremoniously washed it downstream.

In the early fall period especially, topwater baits are popular with many river smallmouth fishermen. However, once again, one of my most productive baits is an artificial more associated with lake anglers—a buzzbait, which I rank behind only the Pop-R as a fall topwater. I generally bring along four rods in my canoe and during the day I change lures frequently. But on one of my rods, I always have a ¼-ounce Hart Stopper buzzbait tied on. On a glorious trip down the James River, I caught four two-pound smallmouths in five casts on this lure and I have buzzed up smallies over four pounds with it. Some river fishermen maintain a buzzbait imitates a baby wood duck about to take off, others claim it mimics an injured minnow slashing across the surface. Actually, I think the explanation lies in the fact that stream smallmouths do not strike at this bait as much as lunge at it. The analogy I use is that a buzzbait whirling through a river smallmouth's domain is equivalent to a friend sneaking up and tapping you on the shoulder while you are watching television. Your reaction would probably be to lurch forward, and that is basically what a bass, safely ensconced in its sanctuary, does when a buzzer comes churning right over its head.

Just as few river smallmouth anglers employ a buzzbait, even fewer use another lake standard—the Carolina rig. I have been using this getup more and more on rivers, especially on heavily fished sections or on any stretch of river with deep

The autumn months typically bring outstanding fishing in the New.

pools. A Carolina-rigged lizard or grub is stupendous bait for deep-water autumn smallmouths. I am convinced that these bronzebacks rarely see a lure presented properly on their level, something a Carolina rig enables an angler to do. River anglers like Barry Loupe and myself admit no shame in imitating the tactics of lake largemouth fishermen. To catch overgrown autumn stream smallmouths, you can do the same.

Winter Wade Fishing with Crawfish Patterns and Lures

When winter descends upon a smallmouth bass river, the conventional wisdom is that the fish become too lethargic to strike and that anglers should just wait for spring. Two Virginia anglers, however, take the non-conventional approach. Saltville's Barry Loupe and Roanoke's Blane Chocklett, who operates the New Angle Fishing Company, emphasize that the cold water period is one of the best times, if not the best, to tangle with good-sized bronzebacks. Even more interesting, both individuals believe that crayfish imitations (specifically soft plastic 'dads for Loupe and crayfish patterns for Chocklett) are the best offerings to employ. Also of note, both anglers believe that wade fishing is the most effective way to present their offerings at this time of year. Here are their secrets.

Barry Loupe: Wade Fishing with Soft Plastics

Barry Loupe says that wade fishing gives him the ability to work a prime pool thoroughly and not have to worry about boat positioning. Since the bass often congregate in very specific places during the cold water period, Loupe can concentrate on these areas.

"Usually in the winter, there will only be a few isolated spots that produce on rivers, and that's where the smallmouths group," he says. "If you use a boat, you might have to cover several miles before you reach a productive location. What I like to do, then, is to have four to six places that I know are cold water producers. I will fish the first spot for an hour or so; then, I will get into my car and drive to the next one. I am able to warm up a little until arriving at the next stop and then fish it hard for an hour or so."

Loupe, who has landed numerous winter smallmouths in the four-pound-plus range, says that for this game plan to work, an angler must understand what constitutes prime winter smallmouth holding grounds. For example, his favorite off-season locale on the North Fork of the Holston features a 300-yard riffle, a 70-yard transition area where the water begins to slow, a large ledge than runs across the river, and a 30-yard by 30-yard pool below the ledge. The hole at the tail end of the area has water as deep as ten feet.

Within that pool is a cut in the bank, and that indentation is the hot spot for the entire area. Loupe believes this is true because smallies do not want to battle current at this time of year, yet they prefer locales where that same current washes food to them. Some people label these cuts as eddy pockets, ledge holes, or slack water areas. Whatever they are called, cuts demand the full attention of winter anglers, emphasizes Loupe, especially if boulders or submerged logs litter the bottom. Barry Loupe maintains that a soft plastic crayfish must be worked correctly in order for its bass-catching potential to be maximized.

"I have four main ways to work a bait in the wintertime," he says. "A basic retrieve means you slowly drag this bait across the bottom. Another common retrieve is to bring the bait back in slow hops. But the two best ways, especially if the fish are sluggish, which is often the case, are to 'squeeze' and to 'shake' the crayfish. For the squeeze retrieve, I merely compress my rod handle. Doing so makes the lure sort of shimmy in one place. You can practice this technique by making very short casts into shallow water. You will notice that when you compress the rod handle, the crayfish moves ever so slightly, and sometimes that's all it takes to convince a bass to strike."

For the shaking technique, the Old Dominion angler merely raises and lowers his rod tip a few inches. This slight movement causes the fake 'dad to slowly rise and fall in the water. The guide says that a two-inch plastic crayfish duplicates the size of the majority of these crustaceans in a stream. He rigs a crayfish Texas-style with a 1/8-ounce bullet sinker. Sometimes he splitshots the bait (employing one to three BB-sized splitshot, depending on the current). Generally, he places the splitshot about a foot from the fake crawdad, but if the bass are very lethargic, Loupe situates the splitshot adjacent to the lure itself. This causes the claws of the crawfish to become erect and undulate in the water.

Barry Loupe has a series of maxims that he holds dear for winter river smallmouths. First, the guide says that smaller lures will typically outperform bigger baits. The fish "don't want a big mouthful," he emphasizes. Second, a rise in water temperature of a few degrees will make for great fishing. Smallmouths are more likely to feed, Loupe explains, if the water temperature increases from 39 to 41 degrees than if the water temperature holds steady at 46 degrees. Third, winter river smallmouths don't generally take bait on the fall or when it is lifted off the bottom. Expect most of your strikes to come when the lure is motionless or barely moving along the bottom. Finally, cultivate a positive approach to winter river angling. Loupe relates that he and friends have experienced days when they caught smallmouths in the two-pound-plus range every few minutes. The fishing action can be just as hot in the winter as it can be during the warm water period. But remember also that there will be days when bites occur very infrequently. Loupe employs very basic tackle in the winter. He uses a 6 ½-foot medium-action spinning rod because the longer rod gives him excellent control and feel, and excels at casting small lures. Clear eight-pound test is his line choice.

The guide sums up his feelings on winter fishing by saying, "[Winter] is definitely the best time to catch your biggest river smallmouths of the year. The fish are easy to find and there is very little fishing pressure. Don't be worried about the fish having a slow metabolism. When they do feed, they will hit a properly presented lure."

Blane Chocklett: Sight Fish in the Afternoon

Blane Chocklett prefers afternoon outings because the water is at its warmest.

"On a relatively warm winter afternoon, smallmouths will leave the main channel area and move to a shallow flat that is adjacent to it," explains Chocklett. "The fish will often be in four feet of water or less, and I can actually see them moving about, looking for crayfish or other food, which are also more active now than at any other time of the day. As I wade, I like to sight fish for those bass. I think the key to catching these smallmouths is to work a fly slow, deep, and thoroughly. Many times I will have to make numerous casts to one fish before it will take."

Chocklett especially targets flats that are four to five feet deep and that lie in the tail ends of pools. If the bronzebacks are not on the flats, Chocklett says he checks out the main channel. This is a time when an angler's previous knowledge of a stream is crucial. The bass will be hovering in areas not easily spotted, such

Winter wade fishing can be quite productive on the New River.

as drop-offs in the main channel as well as places where the channel bends in toward the bank.

The Virginia guide recommends a six- to eight-weight, nine-foot rod and a sink tip line, specifically one that descends about five inches a second. For this deep-water fishing, the long rodder likes a five-foot leader. Size four crayfish patterns are excellent choices. The former fly shop owner also suggests wrapping lead around the hooks to help these flies sink faster or to use pre-weighted flies. Some anglers use bead heads on their flies, as well.

Barry Loupe and Blane Chocklett may go about enticing cold water river smallmouths with different rods and offerings. But there is a common thread to their winter fishing philosophy. They both agree that the cold water period is the prime time to catch some of the biggest river smallmouths of the year and that crayfish look-alikes are among the best imitations to do so.

The Adventure of Fishing for Whitewater Smallmouths

I had not been aboard the raft for more than a few minutes when the first Class IV rapid loomed: roiling, rambunctious, and seemingly eager to swallow the entire contents of the raft like some insane mythological god. My increasing distress surely must have been similar to that of Odysseus when he peered into the gigantic whirlpool that threatened to swallow his ship and crew. Above the increasing din, Brian Hager, a guide for Mountain State Anglers in Lansing, West Virginia, shouted.

"Quick, make a few casts before we hit the rapid!"

It was quite obvious to me that we were indeed going to "hit" the rapid, but shouldn't we be doing something to save ourselves. Not wanting to look like a wimp, I flung my three-inch grub toward the approaching maelstrom. Seconds later, I was surprised to feel resistance on the line, and a moment later I was shocked when a two-pound New River smallmouth soared heavenward.

"Big smallmouth stack up on the lip of a major rapid," yelled Hager. "Fire another one in there!"

I did so and a twin to the first fish engulfed the grub. Releasing that bronzeback, I was preparing to make another cast when again Hager's voice rose above the roar of the rapid.

"I can't hold the raft here anymore, the current is too strong!" he screamed. "Sit down and hang on. We're going through!"

The pair of smallmouths had temporarily distracted me from the rapid, but now that we were upon it, I realized just how large the beast was. Boulders lay in great profusion to our left and right, and it was obvious that Hager was going to have to bob and weave the raft through the labyrinth like a halfback slithering his way through a defense. With the sensation that I was about to throw my life away, I stowed my rods under the raft's frame and dug my hands into my seat cushion. When the first wave of the rapid reared up and slammed me in the face with a wall of water, I barely had enough time to gasp for air before the second wave did the same.

Opening my eyes, I saw that our craft teetered on the edge of a precipice, for we had hung up on a ledge some half dozen feet above a hydraulic—a place where the water is forced to a higher level by the kinetic energy of the current. Meanwhile, the water rushed around us; the river seemed almost like a live creature, pulsing, throbbing, and heaving against our boat. Hager dug his oars into the water column; the craft groaned, tottered, and then, like a bull released into the ring, broke free and plunged downward into the heart of the rapid.

Instantly, a huge boulder appeared to our left. Hager purposefully and lightly "kissed" the rock, pivoted the boat around backwards with the agility of a ballet dancer and squeezed us between two more boulders where the current was coursing through.

Rafting for River Bass

Before you take a journey down a whitewater river such as West Virginia's New as it flows through the New River Gorge, be sure you understand that there is some element of personal risk. Generally, Class I and II rapids present little problem to canoeists with intermediate paddling skills. But Class III and above rapids can cause serious problems for even advanced canoeists. I am a veteran river runner, but I will not attempt to canoe any stream that flaunts Class IV and above rapids. For that matter, any section of a river that sports more than one Class III rapid gives me pause.

Rafts, however, are ideal for white water; when manned by a competent guide, these craft are marvelous and safe modes for carrying you through rough sections. Still, you should realize that the possibility of danger does exist on any trip with major rapids. For that matter, any size rapid that appears overly challenging should be portaged.

The veteran guide then once more swung the boat around, sending us safely into the pool below the Class IV. Glad to emerge unscathed, I was content just to begin to breathe normally when Brian's voice again rang out.

"C'mon, what are you waiting for," he laughed. "The second best place to fish is the pool just below a major rapid. Get some casts in, I can't hold the boat here forever."

A little shakily, I tossed a tube bait into the swift water at the bottom of the rapid. And as was true at the top of the whitewater, I was surprised, though not as much as I was earlier, when a mossyback mauled the lure. This fish went around fifteen inches, leaping and cavorting numerous times before I brought it to the boat. The New River calmed itself for a little while after the Class IV, and Hager and I cruised through pools studded with boulders. Many of those huge rocks held smallmouths behind them, and some more nice fish fell for lures like Heddon Tiny Torpedos, Rebel Pop'Rs, and crayfish-imitating crankbaits.

I also was able to appreciate the beauty of the New River Gorge, which extends some fifty-three miles from Hinton to approximately a mile below the New River Gorge Bridge on Route 19. Established in 1978, the New River Gorge National River, as it is officially known, has become a major destination for Americans who relish whitewater fishing or rafting. The first thirty miles or so of the gorge are fairly navigable. But below Thurmond, the river metamorphoses into a regular wildcat of a stream with Classes I–V rapids speckling the New. Overall, this southern West Virginia river drops an incredible 750 feet from Bluestone Dam to Gauley Bridge. In comparison, the Mississippi descends 1,428 feet from Minnesota to the Gulf of Mexico. Doug Proctor, former managing director for Class VI River Runners, deeply appreciates the charms of the gorge.

"I have been down the New River Gorge thousands of times, and it still is an exciting place for me to experience," he says. "There is so much energy in the river itself and in the guests that we take down it. When people encounter

Rapids Rating System

Class I: Moving water with few riffles and small waves. Few or no obstructions.

Class II: Easy rapids with wide channels and waves up to three feet. Some maneuvering is required.

Class III: Rapids with high, irregular waves capable of swamping an open canoe. Narrow passages require complex maneuvering. Scout from shore.

Class IV: For advanced paddlers only. Intense, powerful, but predictable rapids requiring adept boat handling. Group assistance for rescue is often required. Scouting is a given.

Class V: For expert rafters only. Long, obstructed, and violent rapids. There are precipitous drops that may contain large, unavoidable waves and holes. Rescue is difficult, even for experts.

Class VI: Extreme rapids for teams of experts only. Consequences of errors are very severe. Rescue may be impossible.

the gorge for the first time, they often tell me what an exhilarating time they had. I am really fortunate to live in an environment such as this. The wooded mountainsides, the cliffs, the hawks, the wildlife, and so much more make rafting the gorge unique. And the small-mouth bass fishing is some of the best available, anywhere in the country."

Just when I had become content to cast to boulders in the clear, deep pools with the mountains as an aesthetically pleasing backdrop, Hager called upon me to batten down yet again. Surely, another rapid as bad as the first was not coming up. The guide then told me that a Class V rapid was about one hundred yards downstream, and that we would now have some real fun. Having had my quota of fun for the day, perhaps even for the year, I asked him how challenging the looming rapid was.

"We won't get through it as easily as we did the other one. Still, we shouldn't have any problems," he said.

> **Planning a Trip with Class VI River Runners in Lansing, West Virginia**
> Mountain State Anglers, which is part of Adventures on the Gorge, offers a wide variety of outdoor activities besides rafting and fishing expeditions. Camping, kayaking, rock climbing, mountain biking, and outdoor workshops (some specifically for women) are among the other offerings. All forms of activity can be tailored to include multiple days afield. For more information, contact Mountain State Anglers at: Ames Heights Road, PO Box 78, Lansing, WV 25862; (800) CLASS-VI; www.raftwv.com. For more information on planning a trip to West Virginia, contact the Southern West Virginia Convention & Visitors' Bureau at (800) VISIT-WV.

Hager then plotted our course through the rapid and told me what my fishing strategy should be. I had already learned that smallmouths congregate at the tops of rapids, but I still didn't understand why. The guide explained that whitewater smallmouths seek out seams of relatively calm water above and below rapids. These seams are sandwiched between faster water, and smallmouths race out from them to grab prey careening by. For example, seams sometimes exist on the far sides of the river above a major rapid. Bass will hold in these areas and periodically dash out into the mid-river current to snare a minnow or a dislodged crayfish or hellgrammite.

Below a rapid, the areas of quiet water often take the form of eddies. These areas, where the current reverses back upon itself, are natural haunts of active bass. Minnows, crayfish, hellgrammites, and aquatic and terrestrial flies become trapped in these backwaters. Smallmouths make quick work of this prey, which

Hot Lures and Flies for Whitewater Smallmouths

When fishing current breaks behind boulders or cuts in the shoreline, guide Brian Hager opts for topwaters, minnow plugs, and medium running crankbaits. Since snags and lost lures are inevitable when you fish in swift current, the guide ties on inexpensive lures that can be easily replaced. Good fast water choices include three-inch Kalin grubs on ¼- to 3/8-ounce jigheads and Venom four-inch salt impregnated tubes on ¼-ounce heads. Plan to retie often because of the abrasive nature of this rocky habitat.

For trophy bass, Hager lists the jig and pig as a top artificial. In highland smallmouth streams, a trophy bass typically means smallmouths four pounds and over. Many inexperienced river fishermen think that they have to downsize their lures, even when they are after big fish. The old stereotype that the smallmouth has a "small mouth" still, unfortunately, lives on. Hager says that ¼- to 3/8-ounce jig and pigs are standard on the river, for they will entice bigger fish and stay down in the current better than smaller ones will. The Mountain State guide recommends that the plastic trailer be salt impregnated and come in natural colors such as pumpkinseed, green pumpkin, brown, or orange. Hager says that long rodders often seek out guided trips down the New River Gorge. Productive whitewater patterns include three-inch white streamers and weighted two-inch tan crayfish patterns. For the slower moving sections, try poppers and deer hair bugs.

Angling for whitewater smallmouths can be a real adventure.

is also why a lure or fly tossed into an eddy often brings such a vicious strike. Hager and I made our way through the Class V rapid that day, and since that time I have enjoyed many other trips down the New River Gorge. West Virginia's New River is not the only whitewater stream in America. The nearby Gauley also offers swift water smallmouth action, and sections of the James River in Virginia and the Potomac in Maryland, just to name a few streams, are known for their whitewater bassing. In fact, many rivers across the nation have stretches of white water, and these sections are often the least fished (and harbor the biggest smallmouths) on the entire river because of those rapids. But perhaps no river in the country can boast the New's unique combination of big smallmouths, a mountain gorge, and intense white water. If you want to experience an entirely different kind of fishing, a visit to this rapid-filled smallmouth river is very much in order.

The Adventure of Whitewater Rafting

A certain picture of my wife Elaine and me truly spoke the proverbial thousand words. I am not sure if it was taken when our guide took us over Upper Keeney and the raft almost rammed Whale Rock or when we surfed through Upper Railroad and negotiated both the Big Hole and the subsequent "enders and pop-ups." Or perhaps the photograph was snapped when we galloped through the aptly named Surprise and what the guide called its "pyramidal breaking wave" or when our craft squeezed its way through the narrow and ominous Greyhound Bus Stopper and managed to avoid the perils of its "keeper hydraulic."

In any event, our expressions—displaying a mixture of fear, shock, anticipation, determination, and most of all, the look of two people experiencing a rollicking good time—were recorded for all time. Only a few experiences on the planet exist that can create such a wellspring of emotions, but certainly one of them is a trek through the Grand Canyon of the East, also known as West Virginia's New River Gorge in the southern region of the state. The New River Gorge spans fifty-three miles from the historical town of Hinton to the New River Gorge Bridge (the world's second largest single arch span) at Fayette Station. It features 320 million-year-old sandstone and shale formations, a 700- to 1,300-foot-deep canyon, some 70,000 acres of National Park System wilderness, and perhaps the best whitewater rafting this side of the Rockies.

Basically, adventurers can select from three possible jaunts down the gorge and can spend one to five days within this wilderness. The three major trips are Glade Creek to McCreery, McCreery to Thurmond, and Thurmond to Fayette Station. Nothing more daunting than Class II to III rapids dot the Glade Creek trek, and the mountain scenery is nothing short of spectacular. This section is no place for even an expert canoeist, but professional rafters can handle the

Glade Creek journey with ease. Numerous boulders speckle this part of the river, and they are ideal for sunbathing, shore lunches, and just relaxing. The lunches that rafting companies prepare deserve further mention. You have not lived until you have partaken of a four-star meal atop a checkered tablecloth that has been draped over a boulder millions of years old.

For the ultimate in thrills, try rafting the New River Gorge.

A second option is to combine the McCreery and Thurmond floats, a trek that necessitates an overnight stay on the river. The first day gives participants a chance to become attuned to the numerous Class II and III rapids, which hopefully prepare them for the Class IV and V rapids of day two. Although the thrill of white water is obviously an important aspect of this trip, for me the highlight has always been spending a night outdoors in the gorge. Watching the moon rise above the rim of the canyon and then seeing the stars come out, shining in the crisp, cool mountain air, well, what more can I say. In this age of streetlights, nightlights, and stoplights on every corner, the gorge gives us the chance to gaze into the night sky like our ancestors did. Mornings are special as well, as the fog lifts from the New while newfound friends huddle around a campfire as breakfast cooks.

The third possible outing is to undertake the Thurmond to Fayette Station junket by itself. This excursion features some of the most heart-pounding Class IV and V rapids of the entire gorge, especially famous ones like Millers Folly, Double Z, and Upper and Lower Kaymoor. Just be sure to stay on the left side of the main chute of Miller's Folly, avoid the undercut rock at the bottom of Double Z, and run river left on Upper and Lower Kaymoor. Thank goodness for the well-qualified rafting company guides that intimately know these rapids and the best passageways. All we have to do is hang on and have fun when we run the rapids.

The allure of whitewater rafting is not the only reason to visit the New River Gorge. The mountain terrain also lends itself to hiking, camping, rock climbing, mountain biking, bird watching, and horseback riding. Various businesses cater to individuals who like to indulge in those activities. History buffs like to visit the old coal and railroad towns of the gorge area, and the region hosts numerous bed and breakfasts, country inns, historical sites, state parks, and much, much more. The Mountain State's New River Gorge just may be the premier outdoor destination in the Eastern United States.

Your Best Fishing Buddy Might Be Your Own Child

As my then-thirteen-year-old son Mark and I were carrying our canoe back to the car after a day floating Virginia's James River, I thought about the changes that were taking place in his life. The faintest hint of a mustache was starting to form above his upper lip. His voice was beginning to deepen (although many days his crackling vocal cords had trouble deciding whether they belonged to an eight- or a thirty-year-old), and he was outgrowing his clothes (especially his shoes) at an astounding rate. But the biggest change, and the one most thrilling and satisfying to me, was that more and more he wanted to be by my side when I went fishing. No matter how many close fishing friends you have, if you decide to introduce your kid to this most wonderful of pastimes, you may very well find that your best fishing buddy can be your own child.

How to Turn a Kid on to Fishing

I first began to take Mark fishing when he was four years old. These excursions were frequently quite short, usually lasting less than forty-five minutes and involving very little actual fishing. Most of the time was spent snacking, rock throwing, tree climbing, and overturning stones along the shore. My son had a good time doing those things, though, and he began to associate fishing with fun and exploration. I believe one of the worst things that an adult can do is to instill an ambition to catch big fish from big lakes into a little kid. At age thirteen, Mark still had no desire to target trophy fish. He wanted numbers of fish, and he was not particular about whether they were black bass or bluegills, stripers or sunfish, crappie or chubs. And the more often they bit, the happier he was. This, I think, is true with most budding anglers.

Another decision to make is where to go. Ponds and small streams are probably the best bets. Ponds are practically omnipresent across American's landscape, and many landowners will grant access to them, especially if you tell the property owner that you are looking for a place to take your children fishing. Small creeks are likewise a sound choice. From his earliest days, Mark has liked to wade fish with me. A number of sunfish species populate this country's streams, and they bite willingly throughout a summer day. Another plus of wading a creek is that you can easily show your kid where all game fish like to locate. The primary fish holding areas on creeks also exist on major lakes and rivers—for example, rocks, laydowns, brush piles, and current breaks.

Your best fishing buddy can be your own child.

How Fishing Can Make Your Child a Better Student in School

Ponds and small streams are marvelous learning laboratories. Since his earliest trips with me, Mark was intensely interested in all the little beasties that dwell in and along a stream. He loved to seine for minnows, crayfish, hellgrammites, and aquatic insects, and I worked with his enthusiasm to teach him about the outdoor world. He knew firsthand about the beauty of nature and the importance now and in the future of clean air and water. But my son was also aware that every day in every little section of water, dozens of creatures play out real life and death dramas, busily chasing, killing, and consuming each other. He has seen snakes swallow frogs alive, bass savage damselflies, and ospreys scoop up baitfish. And he has experienced the satisfaction of releasing a bass or a trout unharmed to thrill another angler on another day. I believe that these lessons helped make Mark a more informed student in high school and a better steward of the environment.

Choosing a rod and tackle for your child

Gary Dollahon, director of marketing communications for Zebco Quantum, says parents have several options concerning fishing outfits.

"If you feel that you and your child, say a four- to six-year-old, will only be casual anglers, then I recommend going with an inexpensive packaged outfit," says Dollahon. "An outfit like this will plant the seed for fishing enjoyment and give your child a totally functional but inexpensive rod and reel."

"If, however, the child is a little older, say six to nine, and a little more interested, then I would suggest a plastic spincasting reel with a drag. This outfit is a step up in quality, but not too expensive. Believe me, you will see a lot of things — rods, shoes, clothes — fall overboard when you fish with a kid."

For older children and/or those who have developed a real interest in the sport, Dollahon suggests that parents buy their offspring a one piece spinning rod with a matching reel that has at least one ball bearing. Regarding lures, Dollahon says that an inline spinner is a standard choice for a kid. Spinners entice everything that swims, including some bigger fish. Besides spinners, I used to let Mark throw small crankbaits and topwaters. To make these baits safer, and to prevent frustrating snags, I usually clip off one or more of the trebles.

When to Move a Child's Fishing Interest Up a Level

One summer, Mark was ready to go fishing all day with me. Previously, we had confined our trips to short getaways to nearby ponds or three- or four-hour river floats. Of course, every child's maturity and interest levels are different and forcing a kid to spend too many hours outdoors could turn him or her off for a long time, even permanently. The obvious solution is to let your youngster determine just how long he wants to go fishing with you. For instance, the previous summer Mark expressed a willingness to go camping. After discussing the matter, the two of us decided to take an overnight float fishing trip. I was worried about his attention span and his stamina, but, in short, we had a marvelous time together. The point here is that Mark himself was ready and enthusiastic to expand his angling boundaries. If he had not been so, the trip likely would have been a very miserable one for us both. My son is now grown and is a casual angler but a passionate conservationist. I attribute his love of the outdoors to our early angling adventures together. Ultimately, kids have to find their own ways through life. But I do know that I found a brand new best fishing buddy, and that I treasure the time I spent outdoors with him. The same can possibly become true for you and your child.

Birding by Boat

As my wife Elaine and I toted our canoe down to the stream just before dawn, we paused to listen to the sounds of the night birds commingling with those of the day. On the far bank, a screech owl was whistling its eerie melody while a nearby whippoorwill was chanting its name a dozen times or so. On our side of the river, the prototypical early riser, the Carolina wren, was already belting out its "tea-kettle, tea-kettle, tea-kettle," and a tufted titmouse soon joined in, urging listeners to look for "Peter, Peter, Peter." Soon afterwards, I recognized the notes of a goldfinch, wood thrush, and Louisiana waterthrush. During our day, my spouse and I either saw or heard some two dozen avian species.

Like many outdoor enthusiasts, I enjoy the traditional bird watching junkets to forests, fields, and mountain peaks. But for many years, I have combined two of my favorite outdoor pursuits, river smallmouth fishing and canoeing, with bird watching to further enrich the time I spend on the New River and other streams. Here are some how-to and where-to tips for you to do the same.

How to Bird an Upland River

Numerous kinds of habitat will attract birds on an upland river, but among the most reliable are pools or large eddies, water willow beds, sycamore or silver maple shrouded banks, tributaries, and transition habitats. Mallards, wood ducks, and Canada geese frequent pools and large eddies, particularly if they are adjacent to bends or curves in a stream. For example, when you approach an outside bend, maneuver your craft close to the bank and cease paddling. As you drift slowly, you may be awarded with a glimpse of a mother woody and her young feeding along the shoreline.

A water willow bed is another oasis for wildlife. Great blue herons and green herons stalk the edge of this habitat, just as smallmouth bass and sunfish cruise the adjacent water — all looking for minnows, sculpins, crayfish, and any hapless terrestrial creature that has blundered into the water. Red-winged blackbirds and common grackles often forage in the middle of these beds. A bank lined with sycamores, silver maples, ironwood, and other trees is perhaps my favorite place on a river to bird. The bird I look most forward to hearing is an orchard oriole. Listen for his warbling "look here, what cheer" and other notes, and look for his chestnut-colored body and black head as he flits high in the tree tops. Other birds to hark for include pewees, hooded warblers, and yellow-throated vireos. Belted kingfishers will often perch on dead limbs extending over the water.

Birding by boat is an excellent way to enjoy the avian variety along the New.

Where a small stream or spring enters a river is another marvelous place to bird. I often hear Louisiana waterthrushes at such places as well as Acadian flycatchers and yellow warblers. For sheer numbers of birds, transition zones on rivers are hard to beat. Watch for places where mature forest borders a pasture, cutover, or overgrown field. Among avian species you may see or hear are blue-gray gnatcatchers, yellow-billed cuckoos, common yellowthroats, indigo buntings, yellow-breasted chats, and white-eyed vireos. The vireo's "chip-weaow-chip" is a much anticipated song when I paddle near a field edge, as are the insane rantings, croaks, and whistles of the chat.

Splendid birding can take place on rivers whether they flow through rural areas or cities. For instance, two of my favorite places to bird are the pastoral upper New River along the North Carolina line and the James River in the Lynchburg area. This section of the New is known for its population of warbling vireos, and birders often visit just for that species. One summer, five eagles set up shop along the waterway, and ospreys are another much anticipated sighting. Twenty-two miles of the New from where the North and South Forks meet to Independence is a bird watcher's paradise. Forests, fields, pastures, and scenic vistas characterize this section.

On my urban outing, I floated from Six-Mile Bridge in Lynchburg to Joshua Falls. Although the sights and sounds of the Lynchburg area were a part of the itinerary, I tallied twenty-one species of birds, which isn't bad for a late July afternoon. This float and the one immediately upstream (a six-miler from the Scotts Mill Dam put-in to Six-Mile Bridge) are especially good ones to spot Canada geese, mallards, and wood ducks. The Percival's Island Nature Area is an excellent spot on the Scotts Mill junket to find warblers, vireos, and various shore birds.

Binoculars for River Birding

Bill Hunley maintains that selecting a pair of "river" binoculars is no easy task. "The more I bird, the more I think that less is better in terms of cost and size for binoculars," says the Roanoke, Virginia, birder. "If your canoe overturns or you drop your binoculars into the water, you'll be glad you went with an inexpensive pair. Since you will have to deal with the motion of the canoe as well as the natural shakiness that everyone has when they hold binoculars, a lightweight pair with average magnification is best. A good choice is a pair like the Pentax Weather-Resistant Compact binoculars. They don't weigh much (11.6 ounces), and their power (8x24) is about right for river birding."

Decent quality, weather-resistant binoculars usually run around $130. If you opt for a well-made waterproof pair, you may have to spend $500 or more.

How many species of birds can you expect to encounter on a Southeast river? On an early July trip down the James that my son and I took with Bill Hunley of the Roanoke Valley Bird Club, we totaled thirty-one. But on an April or May getaway, Hunley says spotting sixty to seventy different species is not unusual for streams such as the James and the New. Indeed, combining fishing, canoeing, and bird watching is a superlative way to spend a day on a river.

Jerkbaits: The Essential Spring Lures for Black Bass

"Once you find your rhythm, and the bass will tell you by hitting your bait when you have, you can load the boat," said New River Outdoor Company guide Britt Stoudenmire during a fishing trip. "The retrieve might be a twitch, twitch, pause one; or twitch, pause, twitch; or twitch, twitch, twitch all the way back to the boat or even twitch, sweep, twitch."

That day we were fishing for smallmouths on the New River of course, and the correct retrieve was twitch, pause, twitch; and the lure was a jerkbait. And Stoudenmire did indeed load the boat. But we just as well could have been successfully probing a lowland impoundment for largemouths with a twitch, twitch, twitch return; working a water supply reservoir for spots with a twitch, sweep, twitch retrieve, or investigating an upland lake for bronzebacks with a twitch, twitch, pause retrieve.

The beauty of hard plastic jerkbaits (and their soft plastic counterparts) is that they excel not only as a wintertime bait but also as a spring one, especially when black bass have long since left their winter patterns but have not fully started to spawn, which for anglers can bring frustration but also opportunity. This is why the versatility that hard and soft jerkbaits bring can make them the best transition lures.

Which Category of Jerkbait to Use

Lawrence Taylor, public relations manager for PRADCO, explains which category of jerkbait to use.

"Hard plastic jerkbaits aren't the best choice in the spring when the bass are exceptionally deep, as no company's jerkbaits will consistently go down and stay at depths greater than 15 feet," he said. "The Rebel Spoonbill, for example, tops out at about 10- to 12-feet.

"For those deeper, more lethargic black bass, regardless of the species or the type of body of water you are fishing, the choice would be a weightless soft plastic jerkbait that is skin hooked with a 3/0 or 4/0 wide gap hook. One spring, for example, I had a great day fishing the YUM Houdini Shad by twitching it slow motion or just letting it sink with no motion imparted."

Soft plastic jerkbaits are also the choice, continued Taylor, when bass are most active in the spring, especially when they are cruising just under the surface, as is sometimes the case early in the pre-spawn period. Then a weightless jerkbait ripped and danced just under the surface can bring some jarring strikes. For many other applications, a hard plastic lure is often the choice.

Hard Baits for Suspended Bass

One of those applications involves suspended and/or inactive black bass.

"There are days when the bass are still suspended but they will move relatively shallow because of a warming trend," continued Taylor. "That's an especially good time to try hard plastic jerkbaits for lake largemouths and spots."

The same holds true for river and reservoir smallmouths.

Jerkbaits are an outstanding lure for overgrown smallies.

"Oftentimes in the early spring, there are windows of opportunity when big, mature smallmouths will chase for a brief period," said Britt Stoudenmire. "These windows are often created by a rise in the water, an approaching front, or consistent, stable, low pressure days. Many times, smallmouths will just not fully commit to lures such as spinnerbaits or crankbaits. This is when I like to employ hard plastic suspending jerkbaits."

Soft Baits for Wind and Current

Taylor relates that when those spring winds gust, as is often the case, soft plastics could make the difference between success and failure on a lake or reservoir.

"If you're faced with a very cold, windy day, for example, if the wind is blowing straight in on a point or bank and the fishing is really tough, a soft plastic jerkbait would be my choice. I'd retrieve it slow motion and let it sink periodically to depths as great as 10 feet, or maybe even deeper, until I found the bass."

For rivers or riverine impoundments, the soft plastic jerkbait can excel in current.

"Ripping these baits along very erratically and then pausing them in a fish's face will often gain a response when the bait stops," said Stoudenmire. "Many times the strike is aggressive and ferocious. A suspending soft plastic jerkbait in current has great action, and when paused in the current, no matter how slight, will often back up on a bass, something they can't stand.

"I also like to dead drift suspending soft plastic jerkbaits, giving them subtle shakes every 10 to 20 seconds. Oftentimes when fish hit a dead drifted suspending bait, it is a very subtle take with the line just tightening. I love a suspending jerkbait in the early spring when the conditions are right."

Where Black Bass Congregate in the Spring

Taylor relates that on lowland lakes and reservoirs, certain locales cause largemouths to commingle.

"Deeper bluffs, wind-blown banks, drop-offs along main or creek channels, and emerging weeds are all good places to find largemouths in the spring," he said. "Of course, the closer the time comes to the spawn, the more likely you will find bass back in the coves, especially around rock rubble or gravel bars."

Ron Giudice of Blue Heron Communications agrees about the importance of coves for spring lake largemouths, but he also emphasizes that secondary points out beyond the coves, especially if they sport small rocks of some kind, can also be real pre-spawn magnets. Also good, he continues, are drop-offs along the main channel, creek channels, and points, plus most anywhere a tributary enters the main body of water; or just about any kind of place where warmer water from a spring, small stream, or runoff enters.

A prudent strategy for working coves and the secondary points just outside of these bays is to begin an outing on the points and gradually work inward. Sooner or later, you should contact the bass. What's more, on your way in you may just encounter early pre-spawn bass, true pre-spawn fish, and maybe even some spawners.

The early pre-spawn bass are the ones most likely to be found on the secondary points and also the fish most likely to head for deeper water should one of those nasty spring cold fronts slam the area. If this last scenario occurs, then a soft plastic jerkbait would be one of the most logical baits to tie on.

River and riverine lake smallmouths are also advancing in preparation for the spawn, stated Stoudenmire.

"Smallmouths congregate in staging areas during this period," he said. "When they are doing so, they are solely focused on feeding, and typically, very close to their spawning grounds. Currents' seams, eddy pockets, warm water influences, and creek mouths are all good examples of places where smallmouths will congregate during the staging period."

Stoudenmire especially likes those warm water influences, having experienced great success probing this type of area, as have I. Once, for instance, on a cold spring day, I noted where a spring was seeping into the waterway. Although I had fished the area a number of times, I had never observed the spring, probably because the summertime vegetation had always concealed it. I ended up catching all the keeper bass that I tangled with that day from that warm water ingress and one just down the bank from it.

Similarly, the mouths of creek tributaries can also send warmer water into a lake or reservoir, but they are not as predicable enticers of black bass as springs are. That's because we have to take into account what type of area a creek is passing through before it enters a body of water.

For instance, a creek entering a highland reservoir might still be running cold from winter runoff and/or because the watershed is extremely wooded.

This type of tributary could actually be dumping colder water into a lake, making fishing the creek mouth a losing proposition.

Conversely, a creek flowing through an agricultural area and entering a lowland lake or reservoir might feature water three to five degrees warmer than that of the impoundment and be a true hot spot for working both hard and soft plastic jerkbaits. All this is why a temperature gauge and a topo map are essential spring fishing tools.

Regarding lures for all these scenarios, sage choices include 4½- or 5½-inch Smithwick Rattlin' Rogues, 4⅝-inch Bomber Pro Suspending Long As, 4½-inch XCalibur EErratic Shads, 3⅛-inch XCalibur The Twitchbait, 3 ¾-inch Sebile Bonga Jerks and Magic Swimmers, Rapala X-Raps in a variety of sizes, and 5-inch Berkley Power Jerk Shads.

Rod, Reel, and Line Choices

Stoudenmire says his ideal rod and reel combination for jerkbait fishing is a G. Loomis 6-foot, medium action SJR722 GLX rod with a Shimano Saro 2500 series reel spooled with Power Pro 20/6 braided line.

"I like a relatively short but fast rod to give a hard or soft plastic jerkbait a more erratic action and to provide quick, fast, hook-sets," he said. "I prefer the Saro reel for its fast 6.1:1 gear ratio, and for being able to work the baits fast. And the braided line is a must for both action and good, quick hook-sets."

Hooks, Sinkers, and Rigs for Soft Plastic Jerkbaits

Slamming a hook through a soft plastic jerkbait requires some specialized hooks, specifically depending on the type of rig you are employing. Some two decades ago, T.J. Stallings, product manager for T.T.I-Blakemore, was one of the first anglers to fish the Bass Assassin Shad Assassin, the initial soft plastic jerkbait to mimic shad, and it and other soft plastic creations have remained some of his go-to spring baits ever since.

"For the drop shot rig, you want the bait to stand out horizontally from the line, which makes the bait more visible and natural looking, instead of hanging limply down," he said. "Our Standout Hook has two hook eyes, which enable you to tie the line to the top eye and run the tag end through the bottom eye, enabling the lure to become horizontal.

"For the splitshot or Carolina rig, my choice is the Daiichi light wire, offset worm hook with 2/0 size for 3-inch jerkbaits and the 4/0 for 5-inch ones. The light wire hook won't hinder the bait's action. For the Texas rig, I want a hook to have a bend at its front, which allows more hook to penetrate. Our Daiichi Copperhead hooks have that quality with 3/0 and 4/0 hooks being good ones for 3- to 5-inch jerkbaits."

Tom Scott of Fishing Complete relies a great deal on drop shotting and favors this rig.

"I drop shot Case Sinkin' Salty Shads and Sinkin' Salty Minnows on both rivers and lakes," he said. "I use Seaguar line 8-pound test and depending on what depth or body of water, I have used up to a ¾-ounce barrel drop shot weight in 30-plus-feet of water, paired with a VMC Octopus hook Size 1 or 4 depending on whether I am using the 3 ¾-inch minnow or the 5-inch shad."

By far, my favorite wintertime bass lure is a hard plastic jerkbait, and a soft plastic jerkbait is one of my go-to summertime artificials for sure. Although these two categories of baits are often overlooked in the spring, there's no reason to do so. Just fish them in different ways and places and in the case of soft plastic jerkbaits, with different rigs.

Contacts:

Berkley and Sebile: www.PureFishing.com

Britt Stoudenmire: www.NewRiverOutdoorCo.com, 540-921-7438

Case Sinkin Salty Shad and Sinkin Salty Minnow: www.CasePlastics.com

Rapala X-Rap: www.Rapala.com

Shad Assassin: www.BassAssassin.com

Smithwick, XCalibur, The Twitchbait, YUM: www.LureNet.com

TTI-Blakemore: www.TTIBlakemore.com

Casting for Recovery...Literally

The worst thing that has happened to my wife Elaine and me in our marriage was her diagnosis with breast cancer in September of 2008. One of the best things that contributed to her revitalization after seven months of chemotherapy and a double mastectomy was her participation in a Casting for Recovery (CFR) retreat in May of 2010.

Beginning in 1996 with four retreats and now offering 46 retreats in 33 states including Virginia, CFR is a national, non-profit organization that supports breast cancer survivors through activities that combine fly fishing, counseling, and medical information to create an emphasis on wellness instead of illness. Why fly fishing, though?

Lori Simon, former executive director for CFR, stated that just being out in nature provides healing qualities, both mentally and physically, and teaching participants how to fly fish helps connect them to the outdoor world.

"The motions of casting a fly also gently stimulate and heal the muscles affected by radiation or surgery," added Simon.

A breast cancer survivor herself, Carolyn Harvey is program coordinator/retreat leader for the Virginia events. She plans a budget, and does fundraising, community outreach, participant recruitment and volunteer recruitment and training. Her introduction to CFR came in 2003 as a participant.

"The staff treated us as royalty and made the experience something to last for a lifetime," she recalled. "I came to a group of women as a stranger and left having made friends that left an impression on my life that I would not forget and that also gave me an opportunity to develop a love of fly fishing. I've volunteered with other organizations around breast cancer and the warmth and fellowship developed between the CFR retreat staff and participants made me want to give back."

Mollie Simpkins was volunteer media coordinator for the Virginia retreats. "I do this because breast cancer awareness and serving the women who have been affected is my passion," she said. "When my mom was diagnosed in 1983, breast cancer was not talked about in polite company. Even eight years later when she lost her life, it was not something that many were comfortable having a conversation about...times have certainly changed for the better.

"I'm just lucky enough that my position gives me the knowledge base to reach out to the media. Working with the amazing people of CFR, both nationally and locally along with the participants and all of the volunteers, has absolutely changed my life and focused my purpose."

What Goes on at a Retreat

Elaine and I attended the May 2011 retreat in Madison County as members of the media. Briefly, retreats last 2½ days and combine fly fishing activities (knot instruction, fly tying, practice casting, entomology, equipment needed, stream etiquette, and finally actual fly fishing) with discussions on the physical and emotional aspects of dealing with breast cancer and the objective of overall wellness. Volunteer anglers handle the guiding aspects, and volunteers in the medical field handle the physical and emotional aspects.

Media members are only allowed to attend the last day of the retreat so when Elaine and I arrived, participants were involved with eating breakfast and taking part in drawings for fly fishing gear. Soon afterwards, the ladies paired off with the volunteer men and women who were to be their guides for the morning fishing at a farm pond. While all this was going on, Elaine saw her guide from the 2010 Virginia retreat, Andy Manley of Fairfax.

"Do you remember how I told you to retrieve a fly," Andy asked when he greeted my wife.

"Strip, strip, strip," giggled Elaine and then both laughed about a man instructing a woman to strip in front of her husband. That type of light-hearted banter is very much a part of CFR retreats, but they contain a powerful emotional component as well.

"I've had three different bouts with breast cancer and still have 'chemo brain,'" said Karen Hines of Virginia Beach. "Last night, I got my best night's sleep since this whole cancer thing started.

Elaine Ingram, a 2010 participant in Casting for Recovery, fly fishes for trout.

"Meeting and talking with other women who have been through what I have been through and who were so supportive of me is the best thing that has happened to me in a long time. I wasn't much of a fisherman before coming here, but being outside and enjoying nature is very healing."

Manley agrees about the emotional aspects—for both the guides and participants.

"One of the most special memories I have took place at my first retreat," he recalled. "My participant was close to 70, had never fished, and was a little unsure of herself when we waded out into a trout stream.

"But then she started catching trout like crazy and became so excited that she almost lost her balance and fell in. Just to see her enjoying the outdoors is something that I'll never forget."

Then it was time for the 13 participants and their guides to go fishing at a farm pond stocked with trout and bluegills. I first observed Manley tutoring Hines.

"I caught my first fish on a fly rod yesterday," Hines told me. "It was a beautiful 4-inch bluegill. I'm going to catch my first trout today."

Soon afterwards, Hines hooked a jumbo rainbow which immediately leapt into the air, threw the fly, and landed with a loud splat.

"Are the other fish going to go away now because of all that racket?" Karen asked Andy.

Soon afterwards, across the pond, I witnessed Rachel Wetherill of Bluemont doing battle with a huge rainbow as guide Marcia Woolman of Middleburg coached her on how to fight and net a fish. After numerous leaps and runs, the trout finally entered Woolman's net and Rachel beamed with delight.

"Last night, the women formed a circle and shared their darkest fears," she told me after releasing the fish, her first ever trout. "I can't tell you how much love and support I felt when that was going on.

"Fishing is a way we women can get close to one another, too. It's something that we can experience with our new friends for the rest of our lives."

I then hear shrieks of joy coming from further down the pond and go to investigate. The sounds are coming from Sara Fought, who is simultaneously talking, laughing, and well, yes, shrieking at her just landed trout, guide Brian Randolph of Reston, and me.

"I'd never been fishing before," she exclaimed. "I thought at best I might catch a little sunfish. But the whole retreat has been about me doing things that I didn't think were possible from being able to survive breast cancer to catching fish."

On a personal note, Casting for Recovery has played a major role in Elaine's recovery. She has developed friends from her participating in the 2010 event. Before CFR, she regarded going fishing with me as only an unpleasant wifely chore not to be endured except every few years. Now, we plan trips together, she regularly orders gear from catalogs, and my wife even ties her own flies, adding to her kit turkey feathers and deer hair from game I have killed.

CFR welcomes donations and volunteers from corporations, clubs and individuals, as participants do not have to pay to attend a retreat. Individuals are turned away every year because of lack of funds. As the omnipresent CFR statement says... "To fish is to hope."

For more information on how you can help: Casting for Recovery: CastingForRecovery.org, (888) 553-3500; Facebook.com/CFRMidAtlantic

Making Sense of Modern Line Types

A number of years ago when braided fishing line was first introduced, my friend Mark and I went bass fishing on a hot summer day when the water was low and clear, and the fish were exceptionally spooky. I had heard about the positive qualities of braid, but could not see it ever replacing mono as the line of choice among angling addicts of all persuasions.

After trying a number of lures and failing to receive a strike, my buddy picked up a spinning rod spooled with braid and began making long casts with a Texas rigged soft plastic jerkbait to a shaded shoreline. Soon afterwards, Mark began catching very nice bass, and I quickly tied on a jerkbait to my mono.

I, too, began receiving jarring strikes, but when I set the hook either I failed to have a solid hookset or the bass quickly threw the hook. By the end of the outing, Mark had caught and released a dozen or so quality bass; my tally was two. I rode home fuming, Mark gloating.

Today braid is part of just about every angler's line lineup, but so are monofilaments and fluorocarbons. And, most importantly, matching the correct line with the best lure for the situation has become a crucial part of fishing for black bass and other game fish as well.

First, here is an overview of the major line types, including both their positive and negative characteristics.

Less visible than braids, **mono** is also less expensive by the yard than other line types. Mono can vary regarding thickness, stretchiness, abrasion resistance, and line strength. Generally, though, mono offers stretchiness which makes it a solid choice for working buzzbaits across the surface or slow rolling spinnerbaits along the bottom. That stretchiness allows fish to more deeply engulf these blade baits, making it less likely that our quarry will throw the hook. This quality is also a plus when a fish is about to be landed and makes a searing run near the boat. The negative is that, like in the earlier anecdote, long casts with mono often results in poor hook sets. Ron Giudice of Blue Heron Communications states that some confusion exists concerning monos (extruded through a tiny hole to form a single strand) and **copolymers** (two or more strands of polymers). "Mono lines of today can have a variety of characteristics, each an enhancement to a particular fishing application, yet all are considered copolymer based," he says. A good example of this is Berkley Trilene XL, which remains a favorite of many anglers, including myself. Another popular mono, Trilene XT, is often the choice for fishing heavier cover as the line is more abrasion resistant than Trilene XL. With the tougher feature comes a line that is stiffer, not really a concern when we flip heavy jigs into brush piles. Mono lines are more susceptible to abrasion, UV, and memory and are recommended to be replaced on reels more often than braided line.

Braids are known for their strength, abrasion resistance, small diameter, limpness, and lack of memory. Braids float, which is why my buddy liked to work soft plastic jerkbaits across the surface with this line and why anglers who heave frogs into dense surface vegetation prefer braid. Conversely, the high visibility of braid makes many anglers shun them in clear water. And braids' lack of stretchiness often results in lightly hooked fish escaping. Giduice informs that a major kind of braid is fused line (the filaments have been *fused* into one solid line), a good example being Berkley Original Fireline which works great on spinning reels because it comes off so smoothly during the cast. Berkley Spiderwire Stealth falls into the category of a braid that offers anglers the ability to cast, say, a jig and pig into heavy brush, and implement a solid hook set without having to worry about line stretch at all. "Spiderwire is also great for ripping lipless crankbaits through grass," says Giudice. "But I wouldn't use this braid for crappie because you could rip a lure right out of a fish's mouth on the hookset."

Fluorocarbon has numerous applications. "Many of the pros are switching to fluorocarbon," says Giudice. "It excels at drop-shotting soft plastics, as the line sinks quickly, and it's also great for working soft plastic baits deep. Because fluorocarbon sinks it's not the choice for topwaters. But fluorocarbon is often used as a leader for braided line because it is clear and has a bit more stretch than braid to allow for a little give on the hookset." Berkley Trilene 100% Fluorocarbon and Berkley Vanish are two of the most popular fluorocarbons.

The savvy angler today may have three different types of line on three different rod and reels.

Practical Application

Guide Britt Stoudenmire, who operates the New River Outdoor Company, has extensive experience with all line types. He uses this expertise in a variety of ways.

"For many bottom baits, such as tubes, jig-n-pigs, worms, and soft jerkbaits, I use Power Pro braided line in 20/6 with a 10- to 12-ft, 12-lb Gamma Edge fluorocarbon leader," says Stoudenmire. "The braided line affords me the ability to make longer casts, and with its non-stretching characteristics, I have better hook-setting capabilities, especially at long distances or when I have slack in the line.

"The fluorocarbon leader is better at abrasion resistance than braided line; the leader also sinks better allowing improved contact with the bottom. Further, it acts as a shock leader, giving me a better bottom presentation. Braid sticks to the bottom, making for a harder presentation. Finally, the fluorocarbon leader is not as visible as mono or braid. This is a plus during all conditions, particularly, clear water ones."

Sometimes, however, Brit opts to employ just one line type.

"For all retrieve baits that include spinnerbaits, buzzbaits, crankbaits, and jerkbaits, I use Power Pro braided line in 20/6 directly tied to the bait with a 30-lb Bass Pro duolock," he explains. "For dropshotting, though, I use 6- or 8-lb Gamma Edge depending on depth because the rig is typically weighted heavier, meaning lighter line is needed for deeper depths. For jerkbaits, I use 6- or 8-lb Gamma Edge fluorocarbon line depending on the depths I am fishing, again lighter line for deeper depths."

Selecting and using line is much more complicated than it used to be, but these additional choices do increase the odds of our success.

Sources

Berkley:
www.Berkley-Fishing.com

Britt Stoudenmire:
www.NewRiverOutdoorCO.com

Silver Thread:
www.LureNet.com

Line Wisdom

Lawrence Taylor, PRADCO's PR director, touts the virtues of copolymer and fluorocarbon lines.

"Our Silver Thread AN-40, Super Silver Thread, and Silver Thread Excalibur are copolymer lines, meaning more than one polymer is mixed together before the line is extruded," says Taylor. "By combining several polymers we achieve a tensile strength and abrasion resistance that a mono line can't. Silver Thread AN-40 is designed to be the perfect all-around line with a high tensile strength and extreme abrasion resistance. This makes it good for all general use baitcasting. While many anglers are categorizing copolymer lines as the exclusive domain of topwater fishing, AN40 is a great line for applications as varied as flipping heavy cover or throwing a shallow running crankbait.

"Super Silver Thread features a small diameter and low memory. It's great for general use on spinning reels and offers the same type of abrasion resistance as AN-40 with the small diameter and low memory needed for spinning applications, for example, shaky head fishing. Our Silver Thread Excalibur has a completely different formulation designed specifically for abrasion resistance. This makes it great for short-line presentations in thick cover, such as flipping brush or pitching to docks. It's best used on baitcasting equipment."

Finally, Taylor relates that Silver Thread Fluorocarbon is a good general use line and perfect for leaders in clear water situations.

Float Fishing the South Fork of the New

As one would expect, the South Fork of the New is a downsized version of the New, both in width, rapids, and water volume. I would also state that the smallmouths don't attain the size of those on the Main Stem (a statement that Kevin Hining, a fisheries biologist for the North Carolina Wildlife Resources Commission, agrees with), but plenty of good size bronzebacks fin this tributary. Having floated all of the last 40 or so miles of the South Fork until it unites with the North Fork to form the Main Stem, I can also attest that all of the excursions have quality brown bass habitat.

Jed Farrington operates Zaloo's Canoes in Jefferson and says numerous junkets are well populated with smallmouth bass. Among the better ones are the following:

Hartzog Ford Low-water Bridge to SR 1159 Boggs Road Bridge (8 miles)

SR 1159 Bridge to NC 88 Bridge (6.0 miles)

NC 88 Bridge to Wagoner Road Access (5 miles)

Wagoner Road Access to US 221 Access (11 miles)

US 221 Bridge to Kings Creek Road (7.5 miles)

Kings Creek Road to Confluence (2 ½ miles)

Kings Creek Road to Alleghany County Access (5 miles)

Bob Bamberg, executive director for the Alleghany County Chamber of Commerce, relates that as part of the New River State Park system, the Wagoner Road and US 221 access points offer canoe in campsites, fire rings, and picnic tables. These amenities are quite popular with river voyagers. For more information, see Appendix A: Trip Planner, page 195.

Provided water levels are summertime normal, you'll usually encounter nothing more daunting than the occasional Class II rapid, and the numerous Class Is and riffles will help send you on your way at a good clip. Here are four of my favorite floats on the South Fork.

Hartzog Ford Road Low-water Bridge to SR 1159 Boggs Road Bridge

Farrington says this junket is a delightful one with a number of heavily wooded bends, some picturesque views, and many superlative photography opportunities. The bass fishing, of course, is not bad either. Also of note is the historical tidbit that the Elk Shoals Campground, which lies on this float, received its name because of the large numbers of wapiti that came to water at the river in the 1700s. This abundance of these big game animals also made the area a prime place to hunt during the 18th century, adds Farrington.

Floaters can put in on either river right or left at the low water bridge at Hartzog Ford Road, though the river left side has a gentler incline. Parking is limited. The first half mile or so of this getaway offers shallow water with the occasional dropoff as you drift by fields and woodlots on river right and the occasional home on river left.

Next comes another low water bridge. On a float with my wife Elaine, she moved to the downstream side of the bridge to corral the canoe as I pushed it under the roadway. Do not try to remain in your craft when drifting under these structures. Doing so could result in a scraped back or other injuries and possibly an overturned boat.

After this bridge, the habitat becomes excellent as a long river right bend occurs and both sides of the river are heavily wooded. I once caught a nice 15-inch bronzeback in this section, a fish that fell for a Rapala Original Minnow. Topwater minnow imitations are good options for the South Fork, as they can be worked in a variety of ways in the often clear water. The clearer the liquid, the faster I retrieve hard plastic jerkbaits. In fact, I was retrieving the Rapala very quickly when the bass mauled it.

After this bend, and another low water bridge, comes a long straight stretch with elodea and water willow beds occurring from time to time. Soon you will come to the Highway 63 Bridge, signifying that you have covered about 2½ miles. A long straight section below the bridge offers little prime habitat, and fields dot the waterway in places. This is a good stretch to conduct hit and run bassing, working the productive dropoffs and then paddling quickly to the next likely locale.

The South Fork then creates a river right curve, which, as is true with most bends, offers quality habitat. On various floats, I have caught nice smallies here, too. Once more, the South Fork straightens and a road parallels the river right shoreline for a while. Homes appear on river right from time to time, but much of the river left bank features trees and great rhododendron. It was on this section that Elaine and I once spooked a mother turkey hen and her poults—a real highpoint of the excursion.

Farrington believes that this portion of the float offers the most fetching scenery—and some of the best fishing—and I agree. For much of this section, both sides of the river are heavily wooded and fields dot the banks from time to time. One rapid of note exists near the end of the junket. A Class I ledge occurs; run this rapid on far river right. This is the only major rapid on the entire float, making this trip an ideal one for husbands and wives or parents and children.

The next major feature is a church on river right; then comes a sandy beach on the same side of the South Fork. Numerous folks recreate in this area; testament that folks still gather in this area to experience the outdoors, just as they did when elk roamed the Northwest North Carolina mountains. Indeed, I have come here in the past just to wade fish. My wife's mother's family, the Graybeals, live in this area. Once during a family reunion we stayed at the Elk Shoals Methodist Campground (which is located in this area) and with the South Fork so close, I succumbed to the temptation to go fishing there. I snuck away for several hours, and no one knew, I think, that I had been gone. I recall catching smallmouths and rock bass on that summer day in 1978.

The take-out is just two miles away at the SR 1159 Boggs Road Bridge. Several low water bridges in the meantime will require portaging, but the fishing remains good with plenty of ripples and water willow beds.

SR 1159 Bridge to NC 88 Bridge

Another really good excursion is the six miler from the State Route 1159 Bridge to the NC 88 Bridge, which is just past Zaloo's Canoes. A long straight flat stretch begins this float, and it's best to paddle quickly through here. Then

comes a river-right bend replete with riffles, wooded banks, and pools. I have caught smallies from this section on a number of occasions.

A Class I rapid also lies within this bend. Run the rapid on far river left. Next comes another section of ledges and riffles as the South Fork straightens. Following on the agenda is a river-left curve, which offers perhaps the best habitat of this getaway. Plan to spend much of your time here. As is typical of most bends on the South Fork, this one contains riffles, dropoffs, downed timber along the shoreline, plus a number of ledges and pools. Expect to catch bronzebacks from the aerated water below these drops. Both topwaters and soft plastic jerkbaits have performed well for me here.

The South Fork then straightens, and, again, like many such stretches, this one is best fished with the run and gun approach. At the end of this elongated section, a Class I looms—run the rapid on far river left.

The last mile of this excursion offers more scattered smallie hangouts, such as a downed sycamore along the bank, a mid-river eddy, a main channel dropoff, and a current break within a shaded bank. Zaloo's Canoes is an easy landmark to spot, and the livery resides on river right. Folks that rent canoes can take out here. Otherwise, float fishermen can drift a short distance downstream to the Route 88 Bridge.

U.S. 221 Bridge Float to Kings Creek Road

Jed Farrington maintains that the section of the South Fork that falls within the 26.5 mile portion of the National Scenic River offers by far the best smallmouth action on the entire South Fork. Of that mileage, 22 miles is on the South Fork and the last four are after the South Fork and North Fork of the New commingle just south of the Virginia line to form the Main Stem of the New.

Although the put-in for the U.S. 221 Bridge to Kings Creek Road (7.5 miles) float is listed in the "New River State Park" brochure that contains the canoe access points, float fishermen must note that the U.S. 221 put-in is on private land owned by New River Outfitters in Jefferson. The livery is located in the historic New River General Store, which lies just a few yards from the bridge. To access the river, sportsmen must have permission from **New River Outfitters.** For more information, contact the livery at **(800) 982-9190** or **(336) 982-9192, www.CanoeTheNew.com.** The put-in is on river left just downstream from the 221 Bridge. Anglers will have to haul their craft down a grassy bank.

Biologist Kevin Hining says the U.S. 221 Bridge excursion is very good for smallmouth bass action, especially in the summertime when the upper stretches of the South Fork may have lower water levels. Nancy Bare, who operates the New River Outfitters, says this section is very scenic and has a reputation for quality fishing.

Most of the first mile of this junket offers limited fishing for smallies, though. Shallow bedrock characterizes much of this mile, and few riffles and dropoffs exist. The river-left bank especially is devoid of cover, so I recommend quickly paddling through this section.

Toward the end of that mile, fishermen will come to a river-left bend that features a heavily wooded bank, riffles, and a boulder-laced pool. This is a quality place to wet a line, as are the riffles that lead out from the bend. Numerous underwater boulders and ledges dot this section. Next comes a river-right bend, and a wooded shoreline characterizes this curve and offers fishing opportunities.

The South Fork then straightens once more and both banks feature assorted hardwoods, sycamores, silver maples and river birches. Yet another curve then appears, this one a river-left outside bend. Any wooded outside bend like this on the South Fork is worth fishing hard—and such is obviously the case for this one.

Inevitably, the stream then straightens and homes and fields dot the river-left bank. Toward the end of this straight stretch lies a deep pool known locally as the Blue Hole. Hining informs that this hole has a reputation for harboring giant muskies. A few casts with oversize minnow plugs might be in order. In fact, I once lost a jumbo muskie in this area; the behemoth sawed off my line not long after the battle began.

The South Fork then makes a river-right bend and within it come a series of boulders, riffles and an easy Class I rapid. Not far below this swift water looms an interesting rapid and a superlative place to fish. This locale features a Class I rapid to the left of an islet, and a Class II to the right. The latter also contains some boulders, so I recommend running the Class I on river left. The Class I has a dogleg type pathway. Paddlers can then drift through—and carefully probe—a series of riffles and rocky pools. The river left bank especially is quite wooded and offers more casting opportunities. Rhododendron also covers the bank in places.

Soon you will come to a red barn on river left; this structure serves to roughly mark the halfway point of this float. No more major bends exist on the getaway, and there are not as many good places to fish. First, quickly paddle through a flat, wide, shallow stretch until you come to an island with riffles on both sides, as angling possibilities can exist downstream from the island.

Then you will float by the community of Topia, which is on river right but not visible from the South Fork. Scattered homes line the river-left bank, and the right shoreline is mostly wooded. A small stream also enters on river right. Another stream will enter on the same side less than a mile downstream. A number of boulders line the stream bottom through here, and the fishing possibilities are more numerous.

On the last mile of this excursion, more and more homes will appear, but you will also drift through some three-feet-deep rocky flats that harbor bass. Look for the dropoffs and occasional riffle and concentrate your efforts there. Next you will run a very easy Class I, which can drop down to riffle level later in the summer. Downstream lies the Kings Creek Road access point on river right. This is an excellent access point, as a gravel ramp and wood steps lead away from the river. Numerous parking spaces exist in a gravel lot. The low water State Route 1560 Bridge also crosses the South Fork here. All low water bridges on the river are best portaged for safety's sake.

Kings Creek Road Float to Confluence

Jed Farrington relates that the Kings Creek Road (Route 1308) float is yet another one that has a reputation for producing quality summertime small-mouth action. At the put-in, make note that two outfitters, RiverCamp USA and Riverside Canoe & Tube Rentals, lie on river right and left respectively.

I have taken the Kings Creek Road float (so named because Kings Creek enters on river right at the beginning of the excursion) a number of times, and I rate it as one of the best on the entire South Fork. Also of interest is that the river serves as the boundary for Ashe County on river left and Alleghany County on the opposite shore. Although this junket is short, just 2 ½ miles, it contains a great deal of quality brown bass habitat. At the start of the float, Garvey Bridge Road (Route 1549) is easily visible on river left and the bank is rather barren and the water shallow. Quickly paddle through this area.

The further downstream from the access point you travel, the better the habitat becomes. Soon both banks become mostly wooded as you leave behind scattered fields and homes, and the pace of the South Fork increases. About

¾ of a mile into the trek, a series of ledges and riffles, which may in high water reach Class I size, appear. All of these riffles offer fishing opportunities.

At about the 1½-mile point, the South Fork forms a lazy river left bend, and a riffle lies near the end of this curve. Two major features mark the next section. The first is a commercial campground on the river left bank. Unfortunately, a great deal of shoreline cover has been removed which bass and other game fish benefited from in the past.

The second feature is one of the major rapids on the South Fork, a Class II that lies at the former site of the New River Forge. According to *The New River Atlas* (a valuable source of information for the South Fork and Main Stem) the namesake forge and dam were washed away in the 1878 flood. The debris from this manmade creation, however, has created excellent smallmouth habitat, and numerous large rocks dot this area. Log jams exist as well. Caution: this rapid can be dangerous in high water or even at moderate flows. Consider portaging.

The New River Forge rapid lies at the beginning of a sharp river right outside bend. The river right shoreline is heavily wooded, and rock and wood cover are common. Be sure to linger in this area and work it thoroughly. More superb cover lies downstream when the South Fork once again straightens. Riffles and current breaks are common, and trees especially cover the river right bank, much of which the New River State Park owns. Only about a half mile of paddling ensues before you reach the confluence of the South and North Forks.

Every time I come to the confluence of the South and North Fork, I like to debark from my canoe and climb the point where the water from the two streams first commingles. Once there I take pictures of the two tributaries uniting to form one of America's best known rivers. I can't help but wonder if explorers in birch bark canoes might have done the same thing during the 1700s. Another little peculiar habit of mine is to paddle up the North Fork for a short distance and make several casts. Kevin Hining and I did so on a July excursion and were rewarded with several strikes.

After you reach the confluence, you need to paddle across the New River to the far river left bank. A very informal access point lies off East Weaver's Ford Road. You will have to haul your craft up a narrow, dirt path that leads down from the road. Parking, such as it is, consists of roadside pull-offs.

Conservation Groups on the New River Watershed

Every watershed needs groups dedicated to protecting it, and the New boasts three major organizations that strive to safeguard the watershed for the future. Their primary tool for doing so is a conservation easement, which the Land Trust Alliance "defines as s a legal agreement between a landowner and a land trust or government agency that permanently limits uses of the land in order to protect its conservation values. It allows landowners to continue to own and use their land, and they can also sell it or pass it on to heirs."

My wife Elaine and I have placed 412 acres of land that we own (140 of which are at the headwaters of Sinking Creek which is in the New River Watershed in Craig County, Virginia) under conservation easement. I hunt on the land, conduct timber stand improvement projects, and could farm the property if I wanted, all of which is permitted under the easement process. Here are three organizations that I have worked with on the New River Watershed and that I strongly recommend.

Blue Ridge Conservancy

Walter Clark, executive director for the Blue Ridge Conservancy, located in Boone, North Carolina, discusses the mission of the BRC.

"The Blue Ridge Conservancy's mission includes the protection of land and water resources in the three North Carolina counties that include the New River and its tributaries—Watauga, Ashe and Alleghany," he said. "In these counties, the Conservancy has protected almost 10,000 acres in the New River watershed. On Pond Mountain alone, which includes the headwaters of the North Fork of the New River, BRC has protected over 2,000 acres.

"Much of the protected land on Pond Mountain is being converted from a Christmas tree farm to natural high elevation habitat which should significantly improve the water quality of important tributaries like Big Horse Creek and Big Laurel Creek. Blue Ridge Conservancy is dedicated to continuing its efforts to protect the waters of the New."

Ben Lucas, associate director of land protection and stewardship for the NRC, says the organization's mission is to permanently protect the land and resources of those three largely rural counties in Northwest North Carolina. Lucas adds that since the founding of BRC, it has protected over 18,000 acres and its efforts have also helped result in the creation of state natural areas such as Beech Creek Bog, Bear Paw, and Bullhead Mountain. BRC has helped Elk Knob State Park expand its borders and also, most notably, was a major player in establishing a 2,000-acre State Game Land preserve on Pond Mountain in Ashe County.

Pond Mountain is an incredibly important addition, continues Lucas, as its inclusion permanently protects a part of the New River Watershed including miles of native brook trout streams in the form of the headwaters of Big Horse Creek and Big Laurel Creek. People who trek to Pond Mountain can see into North Carolina, Virginia, and Tennessee.

Lucas adds that not only does the NRC serve the three counties in the watershed but also the domains of Avery, Mitchell, Wilkes and Yancey.

For more information: Blue Ridge Conservancy: www.BlueRidgeConservancy.org.

The New River Land Trust

I am a proud member of the New River Land Trust (NRLT) and annually do a benefit book signing for the organization. John Eustis, executive director for the NRLT, explains why he works for the organization.

"There are two equally important reasons," he said. "The first is what legacy—in other words, what kind of place/world—do I leave my daughter Graelyn? The second is in my thirties, after several career paths, I realized that I desperately needed to do something for a greater good. This may sound like a cliché, but it is very genuinely how I felt. Helping people with land and natural resource conservation allows me to feel that I am contributing to a better place/world now and in the future. "

Beth Obenshain, retired executive director of the NRLT, says that in 2002, the land trust opened its doors and began actively contacting and educating landowners about conservation. The organization began its work at the same time as Virginia began offering a generous tax credit that can be converted to cash for landowners who protect their farms and forest lands. For the first time, landowners who had long wanted to conserve their family farms and historic properties now had the information and the financial support from the state to make it possible.

"Since 2002, we have worked with the Virginia Outdoors Foundation and other conservation partners to help over 230 landowners conserve more than 48,000 acres, including 25 miles of the New River," said Eustis. "Some of the important properties the organization has helped protect include Mary Draper Ingles' 1772 historic tavern and riverfront farm, and an 800-acre farm and wildlife habitat in the Ellett Valley owned by former Virginia Tech President T. Marshall Hahn. We partnered with the Virginia Department of Forestry to secure around $2.5 million in federal funds to conserve high priority forest land along scenic stretches of the New River in Grayson County.

"We also partnered with Department of Conservation and Recreation's Division of Natural Heritage in protecting a globally rare ecosystem on property owned by the Rordam family in eastern Montgomery County. The property supports several rare species of plants because of its unique dolomite soil."

The Land Trust's work to protect the New River and its watershed was recognized in 2009 by Scenic Virginia with the award of its "Scenic Water Corridor Viewshed Preservation Award." It was the first time that this recognition had gone to an organization in Western Virginia. The Land Trust was also the first in Virginia to partner with the Virginia Outdoors Foundation in creating a "Special Project Area (SPA)" for easements, a designation that allows easements on smaller acreage properties. SPAs like the Catawba Valley are areas of exceptional conservation, historic, and scenic values. The Land Trust has helped establish two more special projects areas in our service area: the Spring Valley historic and watershed area in Grayson County and the Little River corridor in Floyd County, and more are in the works.

Eustis says the New River Land Trust is the only land trust in the state that actively helps landowners find buyers for their state conservation tax credits—often amounting to hundreds of thousands of dollars—at prices higher than those paid to other landowners. Landowners use their tax credits to reinvest in their farmland, restore historic homes, and create retirement funds for themselves and their families.

The Land Trust is a community supported nonprofit with lots of passion and energy for conservation despite its limited resources, says Eustis. The organization works hard to be strategic, using both local knowledge and science to pursue conservation of the region's highest value rural lands. This approach has been generously supported by grants from the Virginia Department of Forestry's Urban and Community Forestry Program. The grants have funded development of a GIS-based model that overlaps commonly accepted conservation factors on top of landownership data. The resulting maps and accompanying database identify and rank high-value Green Infrastructure and conservation lands in the region.

Another major activity of the NRLT has been to conduct a risk assessment analysis for high-priority properties and areas.

"This refinement of the model will forecast which properties are at greatest risk for conversion to non-rural uses," said Eustis. "This prioritization and risk assessment model is being used to target high-value private properties within the region for conservation outreach and education.

"Throughout its history, the NRLT has hosted regular landowner meetings across our service region, educated local and state government officials about conservation easements, and worked with landowners to discern the most appropriate path forward for those interested in conserving their lands. We've worked with farm families who have been on their land since before the United States was created. The NRLT has made history—one that will impact the natural world future generations will inherit."

Finally, the NRLT, which is one of the relatively few land trusts in the nation to be accredited by the Land Trust Alliance, has worked to encourage those future generations to be conservationists.

"Traditionally, the land trust has focused on outreach and education for adults, but in 2010 we initiated projects targeting a youth audience," said Eustis. "It was something that needed to happen because engaging with our region's youth plants the seeds that will help conserve and sustain both the natural and human communities in our region and the entire planet. This work has proven both exciting and extremely successful with hundreds of kids outdoors, experiencing the natural environment and engaging in conversation about the importance of conservation."

For more information: www.NewRiverLandTrust.org.

The New River Conservancy

George Santucci, executive director of the New River Conservancy, says the goal of the NRC is to have a completely healthy and fully protected New River, including its tributaries and headwater springs, throughout North Carolina and the Virginias. Clean water, healthy land, and empowered landowners and individuals results in a watershed where people want to live, work, and recreate.

Main priorities of the NRC include research, advocacy, direct action, and resource development to ensure the financial and human resources needed. Santucci says that some important accomplishments of the organization include the following:

- Stopped the construction of a dam that would have flooded 72,000 acres in the 1970s.

- Helped designate 26.5 miles of the New as Federally Wild and Scenic.

- Worked to add land to the New River State Park in North Carolina.

- Added 638 acres to the South Fork of the New to the New River State Park.

- Continued to defend and protect the New, as was the case when a medium security prison was proposed on its banks.

- Worked with other conservation groups to permanently protect the land where the prison was to be built.

For more information: www.NewRiverConservancy.org.

All three of these organizations are worthy of our financial support as well as being worthy of our time as volunteers.

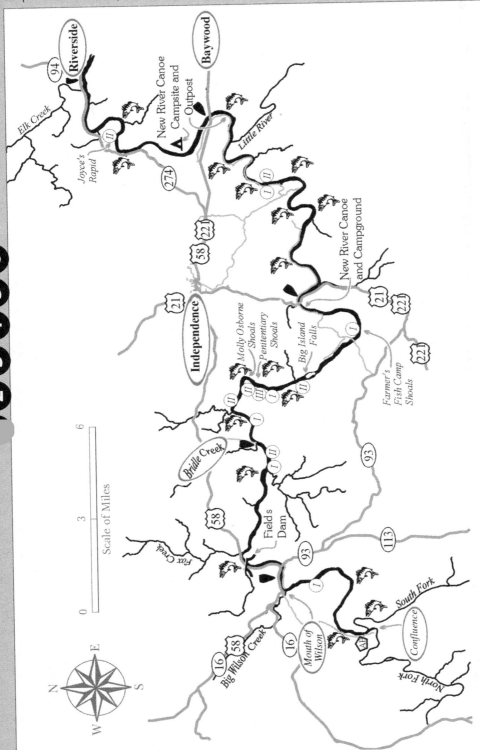

1 Confluence to Mouth of Wilson

TRIP: Confluence of North and South Forks of the New in Alleghany County, NC to Mouth of Wilson in Grayson County, VA

USGS QUAD: Mouth of Wilson

DISTANCE: Five miles

MAP: Page 62

RAPIDS: Class Is and riffles

ACCESS: At the confluence of the North and South Forks of the New, several "community" put-ins lie along the river-left bank off Route 1549. This is a very informal access point off East Weaver's Ford Road. You will have to haul your craft up a narrow, dirt path that leads down from the road. Parking, such as it is, consists of roadside pull-offs.

At Mouth of Wilson, the river-left take-out is near the intersection of Routes 58 and 93, next to the Route 93 Bridge. The take-out is gravel, and parking is limited.

Not far from the North Carolina communities of Crumpler and Piney Creek, the North and South Forks of the New unite to form the main stem of this classic American river. A steep point marks the confluence and at its tip, the waters of the two forks first commingle. The initial time I saw the beginnings of the New proper, I was moved to scramble up that point and gaze out upon the beginnings of a river. I thought about how in centuries past, American Indians, early settlers, and other river explorers had probably done the same thing. Most likely, those individuals had ascended the point to get their bearings, to camp, or perhaps to wait in ambush for various enemies who were also using the river as a means of travel. In some very small way, I was linked to those humans of a distant past, people forever nameless, yet who were more connected to the New River than I and other modern-day river sojourners could ever hope to be. I took some pictures of the confluence to record that brief moment in time and then followed in the paddling footsteps of those who had gone before me.

Another time I took this excursion with Ben Lucas, a guide for Rock On Charters. We had begun the float upstream on the South Fork, and upon arriving at the confluence, Ben spoke about what a moving experience it always is to come to where the New begins. We also both had the idea that we were presented with the rare opportunity to fish three rivers at the same time. We positioned our canoe at the confluence, then made casts into the North Fork, South Fork, and Main Stem before leaving. I would like to report that we caught a big smallie there, but all we tangled with was a very small rock bass. That tiny fish did not lessen the humbling experience of seeing the New at the confluence.

Canoeists can easily negotiate the five-mile excursion from the confluence to Mouth of Wilson in two to three hours while anglers will want to spend a full afternoon on the river. The New winds its way through farmland, pastures, and woodlots; wild animals of various kinds make frequent appearances. Bird life is especially abundant with warbling vireos, a fairly uncommon bird on many streams, being a highlight. Red-tailed hawks, belted kingfishers, wood ducks, and other avian species all dwell along this section.

Anglers will experience fine fishing immediately. A series of deep-water ledges mark the confluence, and good-sized smallmouth bass haunt these rock formations. Ledges like these, which lie in four or more feet of water, offer excellent concealment for smallmouths. Fly fishermen will want to work Muddler Minnows through these lairs and spin fishermen should try six-inch plastic worms and four-inch craw worms.

For several hundred yards after these ledges, scattered rocks and small boulders stud the river and offer limited angling opportunities. Unfortunately, the river is heavily silted through here, as agricultural run-off is a real problem in Alleghany County. Some larger boulders then appear and the depressions behind them provide better fishing potential. Less than a mile into this junket, Grassy Creek enters on river left, and several hundred yards later the first Class I rapid on the New comes into view. During its march through North Carolina, Virginia, and West Virginia, the New River has a well-deserved reputation as a mecca for whitewater thrill seekers. This trip lacks heart-pumping whitewater, but paddlers will undergo plenty of adventure downstream, beginning with the Bridle Creek junket. The river's first rapid features boulders at its center, but numerous passages exist on river right and left, so canoeists should experience no problems.

The next section of this trip offers superlative fishing sport. For several hundred yards, a series of riffles, boulders, and midstream drop-offs dot the New. I like to spend as long as a half hour in this area, working the many current breaks and small pools. Long rodders will find topwater offerings such as Sneaky Pete Poppers and damsel fly patterns effective, and spin fishermen will want to work jig and pigs and crankbaits around the rocky cover. An outpost for Zaloo's

Canoes, a livery with its headquarters in Jefferson, North Carolina, resides on river left and marks the end of this section. Not long after the outpost, the river becomes very shallow, especially during the summer. Both paddlers and anglers will want to hurry through this segment.

The next focal point is the Allegra Development, a series of summer homes about two miles into the trip, on river left. Downstream, a boulder extends from the shoreline to further mark the area. The scenery is mediocre through here, at best, as is the fishing, for the New becomes fairly shallow, especially during the warm water period. Indian Rock, a large boulder on river right, marks approximately the halfway point of the trip and signals some more superb angling. Undercut banks are common on river right, and some barely submerged ledges, drop-offs, and riffles exist in mid-river. Once while a friend and I were fishing below Indian Rock, our canoe hit one of those ledges. The impact catapulted me from the canoe, and I dropped my fishing rod into the water. After I bobbed to the surface from my untimely debarking, I began searching for the rod. As I was feeling my way along the bottom with my feet and gazing into the water for my outfit, I stepped into a drop-off and immediately swallowed some water. While blundering about and trying to reach higher ground, I experienced the undertow, which always seems to exist on the New throughout its length. Fortunately, I always wear a life jacket the entire time I am on any river, so I was in no danger of being pulled under and drowning. But this incident should be a warning to all of the necessity of donning a life jacket and keeping it on, no matter how calm a stream appears. If, for example, I had not been wearing a life jacket and had injured myself when I fell from the boat, my companion would have been hard pressed to save me. More than a rod could have been lost that day.

The next prominent feature is a sign on river left, indicating the beginning of New River State Park, the Alleghany County Access Area. This part of the New River State Park may be reached only by canoe and is an ideal locale for those individuals looking for a place to camp for the night. Facilities include eight campsites, tables, and grills. A pit toilet and drinking water are located nearby. The scenery and fishing are both outstanding throughout the mile of river that the park spans. Photographers will want to take pictures of the heavily wooded shorelines as sycamores predominate, with their leafy canopies stretching out over the stream. Deer Island appears several hundred yards downstream from the beginning of the park. Run to the right of the island and note some gorgeous bluffs on the river-right shoreline. Several riffles speckle the river through here, and it was above one of these riffles that I once dueled with an eighteen-inch smallmouth. The lip of a riffle or a pool, that is the area where the current seems to briefly pause before tumbling over rocks, is an outstanding place to toss a topwater lure. I cast a Heddon Tiny Torpedo to this sweet spot and watched as a brownish streak lunged across the surface to engulf the prop bait. After the fish jumped five times in a three-minute period, I was finally able to land the smallmouth and after taking some photos, I released it.

The view from where the North and South Forks of the New unite to form the main channel.

A long, shallow straight stretch next ensues, followed by another island, which also should be run on its right side. Soon afterwards, you will see a sign on river right marking the downstream boundary of New River State Park. The Virginia/North Carolina state line is about a half mile from this point. The rest of the trip can be easily summarized. A Class I rapid provides some good fishing and is very easy to run; passageways are numerous. Be sure to check out the well-oxygenated water below the rapid. The next focal point is a three hundred-yard long Class I rock garden (Class II in high water) that is very fun to run. Paddlers will want to dally here and explore the numerous paths through these boulders. This area is a super place for long rodders to cast streamers and for spin fishermen to throw buzzbaits as the fish that move into rock gardens are typically in a feeding mood.

Downstream, please note, the last mile of this trip, by which time you are in Virginia, is fairly uninteresting. The major reference point is Wilson Creek, which enters on river left to begin this section. At the end of the float, run to the left of an island to encounter a series of riffles that will speed you on your way. Paddlers will appreciate this break in the flat water, and anglers will want to make a few last casts. The Route 93 Bridge soon appears, and the initial trip on the main stem of the New concludes. Please note that you cannot portage around Fields Dam on river left. Both sides of the river above the dam are in private ownership, but portaging is allowed on the right side, at the time of this edition's publishing.

2 Mouth of Wilson to Bridle Creek

TRIP: Mouth of Wilson to Bridle Creek in Grayson County, Virginia

USGS QUADS: Mouth of Wilson and Sparta West

DISTANCE: Six miles

MAP: Page 62

RAPIDS: A Class II, several Class Is, and numerous riffles

ACCESS: At Mouth of Wilson, the river-left put-in is near the intersection of Routes 58 and 93, next to the Route 93 Bridge. The put-in is gravel, and parking is limited. The river-left take-out is just before the Route 601 Bridge at Bridle Creek. The ramp is concrete, and parking is limited. Virginia and North Carolina have a reciprocal fishing license agreement for this float and the next three trips. Therefore, licenses from either state are valid on these four trips

The Mouth of Wilson trip is a pastoral one that winds by wooded shorelines, pastures, and fields. The float is an ideal one for anglers who desire an afternoon getaway while canoeists can enjoy drifting through in three or so hours. The only uninteresting part of the journey is at the beginning, where Fields Dam creates a mile-long backwater. Quickly paddle through this section, portage on river right at the dam, and you are set for a splendid sojourn on the New.

Immediately below Fields Dam, the fine fishing begins. A series of boulders and ledges run across the river and that rock structure and the resulting riffles produce some ideal fish habitat. This area endures for some three hundred yards, and all of it is worth working hard. Fox Creek then enters on river left, and the cool water from this tributary often causes smallmouths to stack up below it for another hundred yards or so. Numerous large rocks, shoreline eddies, and downed trees provide plenty of places for smallmouths and rock bass to lurk.

"Below where Fox Creek enters is where you can really enjoy some great fishing," said guide Ken Trail of Rock On Charters. "The upper New as a whole receives far less pressure than the New below Claytor Lake. Throughout much of this float, the pace of the water is good, not too fast or slow. My friend and fellow guide Ben Lucas and I have had some incredible days fishing this section. Here's a tip, the Rapala X-Rap is a great lure for fishing this section, especially in the spring."

The view from Fields Dam.

Fox Creek is the only fairly large tributary on the Mouth of Wilson float, but many small creeks and branches enter throughout this section. Herein, lies both a positive and a negative factor. When tributaries enter any river, they tend to bring warmer water in the winter and early spring and cooler liquid in the summer and early fall. This influx tends to attract game fish throughout much of the year as they constantly search for the most favorable water temperatures. If excellent habitat exists below the mouth of a stream (as is true where Fox Creek enters), then angling can be excellent there during much of the year. The downside of the tributaries on the Mouth of Wilson junket, however, is that they typically drain agricultural areas. A fair amount of rainfall will cause the water in these small streams to turn brown, which in turn muddies the New. I have paddled this section a number of times, and many were just after rainfall, or precipitation occurred after I put in. Each of these times I saw the New either muddy, or the stream become that way after the rains. Not coincidentally, siltation from bank erosion is noticeable in many areas. This section is a prime reason why farmers and cattlemen should be strongly encouraged and given financial incentives to leave riparian buffers (areas of trees and vegetation) along a waterway. Doing so would prevent these landowners from seeing their land slowly wash away as well as improve water quality, reduce siltation, and preserve streams like the New for future generations.

The next portion of this float is a must-stop for outdoor photographers. A steep hill rises on river left, and a bluff with small caves resides at the top. A wooded shoreline on the opposite side features rocks and downed trees. This river-right bank is also a fine place for long rodders to toss poppers and hair bugs and spin fishermen to cast Heddon Tiny Torpedos and Rebel Pop'Rs. Afterwards comes a rock shoal and below it a pool. On warm sunny afternoons in this area, I like to cast damsel fly imitations. Damsel and dragonflies populate the New in great numbers, and smallmouths frequently leap from the river to intercept these creatures when they fly too close to the surface. I once hung a large smallmouth in this pool when I cast a buzzbait to a current break just below a rock. Although this micro-eddy had water just a few feet deep, the smallmouth had moved into the current break to feed. The bronzeback mauled the buzzer and immediately swam toward my canoe. Whenever a bass "runs" toward your boat and slack line develops, you are very likely to lose the fish if it jumps. Predictably, the smallmouth went airborne, throwing the hook while I cried out in anguish.

The next major feature of this trip is an island that cleaves the New. Take the river-right passageway, and you will encounter a beautiful cliff and a cave on river right and some marvelous, rocky habitat. This is another wonderful place to take some photos and enjoy a shore lunch. My wife and I also once hunkered down in the cave during a late June thunderstorm. Below the island comes a series of riffles, followed by some shallow stretches and then isolated drop-offs and small eddies. These are good places for fly fishermen to cast streamers and spin fishermen to throw crankbaits and grubs. About four miles into the trip comes another shoal area. The "push water" portion (that is, an area above a shoal where the current picks up speed before tumbling over rocks) is a stupendous place to cast hellgrammite nymphs and black plastic worms and ringworms. Canoeists will enjoy the accelerated speed of the push water as the New moves along at a quick pace. If you are a photographer, debark at the river-right bank and snap some gorgeous vistas. The next major feature is an island; run it on river left where a riffle will speed you on your way.

The last mile of the Mouth of Wilson float is a pleasurable one for outdoor lovers of all kinds. A long rock garden dominates this section, and two small islands dot the river. Guide Ken Trail says that this section is often a highlight of his day. Wooded banks are the norm, and bird life and waterfowl are abundant. An easy Class I rapid, passages are numerous, adds flair to this section, as well. Both spin and fly fishermen can easily spend an hour or more here and canoeists may want to explore the many passages through the boulders. Photographers can consider all manners of interesting compositions with the rock garden, forested shores, river, and sky. Within one mile of the take-out, there is another Class I rapid; run it down the middle. At the end of the trip just above the take-out is the Class I-II Bridle Creek Rapid. If you take the far river-left route, you will avoid the heart of the rapid and experience little difficulty. This is also the best route to the river-left take-out which lies just upstream from the Bridle Creek Bridge. Experienced paddlers who are continuing on to Independence will want to run the river-right side for some whitewater thrills. Providing rains have not muddied this section, the Mouth of Wilson float has much to recommend it.

3 Bridle Creek to Independence

TRIP: Bridle Creek to Independence in Grayson County, Virginia and Alleghany County, North Carolina

USGS QUAD: Sparta West

DISTANCE: Ten miles

MAP: Page 62

RAPIDS: Class III Penitentiary Falls, three Class IIs, and many Class Is and riffles

ACCESS: At Bridle Creek, the river-left put-in is just before the Route 601 Bridge. This area is also known as Cox Chapel. The ramp is concrete, and parking is limited. At Independence, the river-left take-out is several hundred yards past the Route 21 Bridge. The actual take-out is located on Route 700. The ramp is gravel, and parking spaces are numerous.

The Bridle Creek junket is perhaps the premier one on the upper New above Claytor Lake for both paddlers and float fishermen. Canoeists should plan to spend at least five hours on this trip because of the scenery, photographic possibilities, and the technical nature of some of the rapids. Portaging may be necessary. In spring or any time when water levels are high, only expert paddlers should take this excursion. Even when water levels are normal, several danger spots exist. For anglers, this ten-miler is definitely an all-day float.

"This is one of my favorite trips on the entire New River," said guide Ben Lucas of Rock On Charters. "Really good smallmouth habitat exists throughout most of the float. Upstream and down from the Molly Shoals area is especially good because of all the rock cover. The scenery is great, too. The Bridle Creek float is really a snapshot of traditional Southern farm land and a way of life. Even better is the fact that the first nearly three miles of the float is almost entirely protected by conservation easements. That section will look that pristine forever."

One of the most interesting things that has occurred in recent years on the New throughout its journey through Carolina and the Virginias is the rise of a major muskie fishery. In addition to all the sublime smallie habitat, Lucas says that the float also features a number of long, deep rocky pools that harbor jumbo muskies.

The Bridle Creek float begins when you glide under the Route 601 Bridge and encounter an extremely easy Class I. Wade fishermen frequent this area which receives considerable angling pressure. Farmland and scattered woodlots characterize the first mile of the float. Fishing is fair as this section hosts scattered boulders, small riffles, and mostly shallow water. But as you approach the beginning of mile two, the river undergoes a dramatic change as it forms an outside bend on river left. Some local people call this the Osborne Shoals area. In the pre-Revolutionary War period, Osborne's Fort was situated here, and a marker now testifies to that fact. The marker is located next to a white farmhouse that is visible from the river. You can view the marker from Route 711, which runs along or near the New on river left during the first two miles of this junket.

Osborne Shoals itself dominates this approximately half-mile-long outside bend. The bend begins with a Class I rapid, and the fishing above it can be outstanding. On one foggy August morning, I watched smallmouth bass savage minnows among the rocks and ledges just above this rapid. The hapless minnows kept leaping across the surface in often futile attempts to escape their pursuers. When you encounter situations such as this, toss Clouser Minnows or buzzbaits into the melee. On that morning, I only caught one good-sized smallie from this area, but it was exciting to guess where the smallmouths would turn up next as they chased the skipping minnows. The Class I here is very easy to run and passageways are numerous and obvious. A series of ledges and small boulders then appear, and the fishing remains great. I like to spend as long as an hour here working the eddies and pockets below the rock structures. Canoeists will likewise find this area delightful as they scoot in between the boulders. Photographers may want to try to capture the river, its boulders, and the wooded hillside on river left. A challenging Class II rapid/ledge concludes the Osborne Shoals area. Canoeists and kayakers should traverse this rapid on its far river-right side. When you enter the rapid, take a hard right, then almost immediately undergo a hard left to avoid a tricky ledge. Portaging is possible from the river-right side.

The next mile or so is extremely scenic. Hemlocks, striped maples, and Catawba rhododendron thrive along the cool, shady river-right bank. During the summer, no matter how hot the air temperature or how high the humidity is in the mid-river section, a refreshing breeze and cooler temperatures prevail along this bank. Fishing is best along this shoreline in spring; by summer most of it rests in only a few feet of water. The river-left bank is also quite appealing as farmland and pastures predominate. Don't revel in this pastoral setting for too long, however, because the Class II Molly Osborne Shoals looms. Shoal Creek dribbles into the New on river left, and immediately below a series of ledges and rocks dot the stream. You will also spot an island, which is best run on its right side. Molly Osborne Shoals is a very technical Class II at low or normal river levels and a very challenging and potentially dangerous Class III at high water levels or during the spring. Many of the chutes through the rapid cause a canoe to veer to the left. Lucas recommends that paddlers attempt to negotiate Molly Osborne Shoals on its far river-left side. The last chute through here will cause you to skirt the edge of the island's terminus, and you will need to make a hard left turn to avoid some boulders. However, so many boulders and ledges exist before you reach this stage of the rapid and so much fast water courses within, that your canoe may be forced elsewhere. If you are not an expert paddler, I recommend portaging Molly Osborne Shoals on its river-right side.

The reason for this caution is based on several incidents I have witnessed. On one summer outing, I watched a group of eight try to negotiate Molly Osborne. The first canoe capsized when its inhabitants were unable to find the river-left chutes and were forced down the right side. The second canoe nearly broached, banged into numerous rocks, and finally limped over the last drop. The third canoe, manned by two young boys, miraculously made its way through but not before almost tipping over. And the last two members of the party became so confused that their craft become wedged between two boulders and almost tipped over at the precipice. Finally, the twosome righted themselves and made their way through. Seven of these eight people attempted Molly Osborne without wearing life jackets. Only one woman had enough common sense to don her jacket before the rapid. My boat mate and I paddled over to the party afterwards, and strongly suggested that the New River was too dangerous a waterway for paddlers not to wear life jackets throughout its length and especially when major rapids come into view. The group members seemed chastened by their experiences and our warnings, and they did finally put on their jackets.

In this same area, I once saw another example of human idiocy. A lone fisherman was trying to haul a motorized johnboat up Osborne Shoals. The man was wearing chest-high waders, even though the air temperature was in the mid-80s and the water temperature was in the mid-70s. What's more, the individual was not wearing a life jacket as he struggled to tow his boat upstream. This man was performing at least four incredibly stupid acts. First, you should never go boating on the New or any river by yourself; too many things can go wrong, from broken bones to becoming lost or losing your balance and falling in. Second, chest-high waders should never be worn in the warm weather period. You may keep your shorts dry, but if you should slip and become submerged, the water within those waders can very possibly prevent you from rising above the surface. Third, johnboats have no business being hauled through rapids. Even if you should make your way upstream, these craft are not made for running major rapids such as those that litter the Bridle Creek excursion. And, last, the stupidity of not wearing a life jacket is apparent.

The Bridle Creek excursion is an outstanding one for couples.

After Molly Osborne Shoals, you will have several hundred yards of relatively calm water. This is a good place to take upstream shots of Molly Osborne, rearrange your gear, and enjoy some fishing as you pass between Shoal Hill on river left and Buzzard Hill on the right. Coming up next is the Class III Penitentiary Shoals Rapid, a possible Class IV in high water. You may scout and portage this rapid on the river-left side, and I recommend portaging if you and your boat mate are not expert paddlers. Penitentiary is best negotiated by going down its left center side. Be aware of some barely submerged shoals at the beginning of the rapid and a large sharp rock that looms about two-thirds of the way through. On my first trip through Penitentiary, a friend and I maneuvered our way through the submerged shoals in good fashion, and I was beginning to think that we had conquered the rapid. As we passed the aforementioned rock, we barely kissed it. The next thing I knew, the boat flipped and I was struggling to keep my head above water and hold onto fishing rods, which had luckily bounced out of the canoe and into my hands. Fortunately, my friend emerged downstream unscathed and I was able to bob my way through the rest of Penitentiary with only a few bruises and one lost mini tackle box. We went around the rock on its left side, but some canoeists recommend that it should be negotiated on its right. Paddle directly toward the rock, in order to avoid a shoal above this mini boulder, and then make a hard, last second right around the rock. If this sounds technical and challenging to you, you are right. I prefer to portage Penitentiary. Ben Lucas recommends caution concerning this rapid.

Below Penitentiary lies some of the best fishing on the Bridle Creek float, says Lucas, and I agree. A series of ledges and riffles characterize the next half mile of the river. Good flies and lures for this section include crayfish patterns and tube baits as bronzebacks frequently root among the many rocks here. A Class I rapid runs across the river several hundred yards below Penitentiary. Passages are numerous and if you survived Penitentiary Shoals, you should have no problems. At the end of this half-mile section, a large island comes into view on the right; run this island on its left side. The shallow riffles through here are fun to paddle and the area itself is very pretty.

Next comes another island and a series of easy riffles and Class Is for several hundred yards. This island likewise should be run on its left side. Fishing is better here than in the previous area because the water is deeper. Throw topwater patterns such as hair bugs and grasshoppers and lures, such as Heddon Tiny Torpedos, Rebel Pop'Rs, and Storm Chug Bugs. The next mile or so of the river is fairly shallow and easy to run. You then come to the approximate halfway point of the trip, the Virginia/North Carolina line, and Big Island Falls, a Class II. Run to the right of the island as it is heavily silted on its left side. I take the center right channel through Big Island Falls; this is a fairly easy Class II, especially for the New. The next mile or so offers some of the best bank fishing on the upper New. Rhododendrons and hemlocks envelop the bank, which rests in water three to five feet deep. On one dog-days excursion, I repeatedly cast a ¼-ounce Hart Stopper buzzbait to the shoreline and had numerous good-sized smallies maul it. This is an especially good area to fish in the afternoon when the bank is bathed in shade. The river-left shoreline offers pastoral vistas of agricultural fields and pastures.

The next major feature comes near the seven-mile point of the Bridle Creek junket. An easy Class I rapid appears just before Route 702 crosses the river in the form of a low water bridge in Alleghany County, North Carolina. This is a very popular place for swimmers, sunbathers, and wade fishermen. The river then forms a river-right bend for over a mile with a large wooded hill at the beginning. Usually, outside bends offer superlative fishing, but here the water is fairly shallow and angling opportunities are limited to a few deep holes. Farmer's Fish Camp Shoals, a series of small rapids interspersed throughout this bend, is the next important feature. These rapids are easy to run and are rated as Class Is under normal water conditions.

The last leg of the Bridle Creek trip offers limited fishing opportunities and uneventful paddling. The scenery is excellent, though, and I like to make many stops to take pictures of wooded shorelines and of cows grazing along the river. Just before the end of this float, you will encounter one last major island. Go to its left side to take advantage of some riffles to send you on your way. Soon afterwards, the Route 21/221 Bridge appears and several hundred yards later, you will see a ramp on river left and the New River Canoe and Campground on river right. The Bridle Creek journey is one of the best ones on the entire New River.

Independence to Baywood

TRIP: Independence to Baywood in Grayson County, Virginia, and Alleghany County, North Carolina

USGS QUADS: Sparta West and Sparta East

DISTANCE: Twelve miles

MAP: Page 62

RAPIDS: One Class I-II rapid and numerous riffles

ACCESS: At Independence, the river-left put-in is located on Route 700, which is off Route 21. The ramp is gravel, and parking spaces are numerous. The put-in is located directly across the river from a well-known livery, New River Canoe and Campground. At Baywood, the take-out is on river right just past the Route 58/221 Bridge. The ramp is gravel, and parking spaces are numerous.

The Independence excursion is a full-day float for anglers and a long afternoon for paddlers. The twelve-mile journey is ideal for canoeists with limited experience because this is one of the more placid sections of the New. In fact, I would rate this trip as the best one on the entire New for families and inexperienced canoeists. Photographers more interested in snapping scenic vistas than running rapids will also delight in this journey.

"The Independence float is one of the best on the upper New for muskies," said guide Ben Lucas of Rock On Charters. "The deep water holes provide outstanding habitat for muskies."

The first mile of the Independence junket features riffles and some wooded shorelines, especially on river left. It is also at this stage that the New River dips (for less than a mile) into North Carolina for the last time. Also in this section, travelers will encounter a beautiful rock garden where numerous boulders stud the river. This is one of the better places to take scenic shots of the New and surrounding countryside. Route 700 runs along the river until about the two-mile-point, giving wade fishermen access to the stream. But the fishing and scenery really become outstanding two miles in when the summer homes become scarce and wooded hillsides and pastures envelop the New.

Indeed, from this point until a Class I to II rapid metamorphoses at about the seven-mile marker, the river is remarkably consistent in its gorgeous scenery, good fishing, and easy paddling. The stream curves about displaying cattle grazing on hillsides, rhododendron-shrouded banks, wooded shorelines, and the occasional boulders, drop-offs, and small ledges. This is a stretch where you can leisurely cast for smallmouths, idly talk as you paddle, or periodically stop to take pictures. The best place to fish on the entire trip is the aforementioned Class I to II rapid a little past the halfway point. When water levels have dropped, a number of rocks appear and boaters should take care while running this rapid. Conversely, when water levels rise, this rapid turns into a Class II and demands attention. Most of the time, though, this rapid is very easy to run and the best path is always straight down the center. Portaging is possible on the river-right side.

Angler fishing above the only Class I-II rapid on the Independence float.

Above this rapid, boaters will want to linger in order to fish a series of ledges and underwater rocks. After running the heart of the rapid, eddy out on river left and fish a rock strewn shoreline. The influence of the rapid lasts for a hundred yards downstream and all of this stretch offers outstanding fishing for those inclined to throw streamers, nymphs, grubs, and buzzbaits. Shutterbugs and those interested in a break or a shore lunch will want to debark on the river-right island or shoreline here. This is a marvelous place to take pictures of the rapid and the rocky bank on river left. Be aware that a sharp ledge lies just below the island, but it is easily spotted and avoided.

The river next forms a river-left bend and along that bank grows rhododendron in profusion. The rhododendron here blooms in late June through mid-July most years, making that period the most scenic time to take the Independence float. The fishing is steady as numerous rocks and ledges dot the river and provide some marvelous deep-water habitat. On one voyage through here, I saw a farmer riding an ancient-looking tractor to hay his field on the river-left hillside, a scene that could have occurred fifty or more years ago and hopefully will be played out throughout this century. During that same trip, I also viewed an osprey cruising the stream in its never-ending search for fish. One of the great conservation success stories of the past few decades is the return of this raptor to the New. Hark to the whistled "yewk, yewk, yewk" of the osprey and watch for its largely white head and black cheek patch. One of the most thrilling sights on the New is to view an osprey plunging into the river to snare some hapless carp, sucker, or minnow. Scenes such as these truly flavor the Independence float.

Two major features characterize the river between the nine and ten-mile points. A series of sharp ledges, lying parallel to the flow, punctuate the river and provide smallmouth habitat. And several hundred yards later, the Little River enters on river right. After the Little River enters, the New becomes very sandy and slow flowing; and serious fishermen will want to paddle quickly through this section.

The rest of the trip can be easily summarized. Several hundred yards below where the Little River enters, anglers will encounter a river-right bank that is heavily vegetated and offers shade, rocks, numerous laydowns, and superb fishing. This is also a great place to bird watch as scarlet tanagers, acadian flycatchers, and a host of vireos and warblers lend their musical voices to the surroundings. And on the river-left bank during summer outings, look for blackberry vines that grow in abundance. On a mid-July trip, I once stopped there and feasted on ripe, tart blackberries—a river fruit bar that rates four stars. In fact, one of the great joys of floating a river is to occasionally stop and taste various wild fruits growing along the shoreline. I have dined on wild strawberries in May, black raspberries in June, wineberries in July, blackberries in July and early August and summer grapes in September. Vitamin C need not always come from a pill or a can.

Shortly afterwards, several small islands appear along the river-left bank as do a number of summer cabins. The New River Canoe Outpost and Store follows immediately downstream. Expect to see tubers and swimmers along this section on summer days. After passing under the Route 58/221 Bridge, paddle over to the river-right take-out to conclude the Independence junket. This is a must-take trip for families, paddlers, and muskie anglers especially.

5 Baywood to Riverside

TRIP: Baywood to Riverside in Grayson County

USGS QUADS: Sparta East and Brierpatch Mountain

DISTANCE: Eight and a half miles

MAP: Page 62

RAPIDS: Class II Joyce's Rapid, one Class I, and riffles

ACCESS: At Baywood, the river-right put-in is just past the Route 58/221 Bridge. The ramp is gravel, and parking places are numerous. At Riverside, the river-left take-out is near the intersection of Routes 274 and 94. The ramp is gravel, and parking places are numerous.

Guide Gil Gillenwater, who operates Greasy Creek Outfitters, shared this poignant story about the often special nature of a day on the upper river.

"Float fishing is my favorite way to fish because it lets the angler focus on the fishing and lose themselves in the moment," he said. "I've seen friends strengthen friendships and relive the years gone by, business associates grow their association on a personal level and parent and child spend quality time together without distraction in the perfect setting to connect on a level that is often hard to do off the water. One trip that I talk about often was a pair of friends that had been best friends for decades, Pat and Charlie. They fished for two days and for two days they ribbed each other non-stop, laughed and told me every fishing adventure they had ever been on together. Now, Pat was a big guy and he often ran out of distance when he cast, putting his lure into the trees. Time and again Charlie, from the back of the boat, would say 'Well, if you're not getting in the trees every now and again, you're not taking the chances you need to in order to catch fish!' As it were, these two friends fished with me for two days and went home with smiles on their faces. Three days later, Pat called with the news that the two days we spent on the water were Charlie's final trip.

"That may seem like a sad note, but after the sadness, I felt honored to have spent the time I did with these two characters and I gained a new appreciation for Thoreau when he said 'Many men go fishing all of their lives without knowing that it is not fish they are after.' That quote and those two friends' story are staples for my trips now; I want to make sure that while we are certainly focused on the fishing, the fish aren't why we're there."

Except for the Class II, Joyce's Rapid, at approximately the six-mile point, the Baywood float is free of major rapids, making it an outstanding choice for family floating. And from approximately the two-mile point to Joyce's Rapid, the scenery is as fetching as any section of the New. Anglers should allot almost a full day to this float while paddlers can easily negotiate it in three to four hours.

Often the fishing is quite poor around the access points on many rivers, but solid action is available from the start on this junket, says guide Ben Lucas of Rock On Charters.

"There's great fishing within sight of the put-in, which is very amazing and unusual on the New and on other rivers for that matter," he said. "On this section and on the trip as a whole, there are some really nice deep water ledges. In the summertime, I fish those ledges with soft plastics like tubes and jerkbaits and catch a lot of nice smallmouths in the 14- to 17-inch range."

The first mile or so features submerged mid-river boulders and ledges, numerous drop-offs, and a moderate current. I like to paddle out to the middle of the river and cast crayfish imitations upstream to the base of those boulders

The author's wife, Elaine, with a fine smallmouth taken on the Baywood excursion.

and ledges. On one visit, I took a beautiful two-pound bronzeback by doing so. The smallie engulfed my offering while it was in approximately seven feet of water. When strikes occur, they usually take place during the first few feet the fake crustacean travels. This is not a particularly scenic section as trailers and summer cabins line the river-left side, although a wooded hillside adds character to much of the river-right bank. At about the one and a half mile point, an easy Class I rapid appears; passages are numerous. This is an exceptionally photogenic spot as the area boasts some beautiful in-stream boulders and a heavily wooded river-right shoreline. I also have experienced good luck here with crayfish lures and patterns. Below this rapid, I once encountered several North Carolina anglers who had journeyed into Virginia. One of the great joys of river fishing is meeting other sportsmen and asking the proverbial, "Catching any?" The guarded reply is almost always, "A few, how about you?" On the outing that I met the Tarheel duo, I had enjoyed some excellent fishing thus far, but when they asked me how I was doing I replied, "Things are a little slow." Obviously, this was an outright lie on my part and I readily confess my transgression. The only time I tell the truth about my efforts is when I am not catching fish and then I readily admit my failures. I always worry that the strangers I am conversing with will not practice catch and release and will exploit the fishery. I suspect that most people I encounter have the same worry about me and others they meet. In American folklore, fishermen are regarded as notorious liars concerning the size and quantity of their catches. I think our reputation is deserved. I have actually seen friends who were in the process of playing big bass, flip the bail, drop their rods into the canoe, and pretend that they didn't have fish on when canoeists came upon us. These companions were afraid that other people would come back to their "spots." I guess besides being liars, we are also a little paranoid at times.

I also want to add that walleye anglers are the worst liars among the fishing fraternity. The New's walleye fishery has become well-known, but many people, myself included, really do not know how to fish for them. The New has a few devoted walleye enthusiasts who will not only claim that they are not fishing for this species but were also unaware that any fin the river.

At about the two-mile point, notice a primitive campsite on river right owned by New River Canoe and Campground. The scenery through here and for the next four miles is awe-inspiring. The river weaves its way through heavily wooded forests, and mammoth boulders line the river-right shore in places.

Boulders also dot the streambed and create numerous current breaks for game fish and photo opportunities. Some of these boulders, both in and out of the river, make for dandy spots for respites and shore lunches. On summer afternoons, eddies and pools below these boulders are often superlative places to watch hatches take place. On summer afternoons, the damsel and dragonfly hatches especially can be quite heavy and the smallmouths take full advantage of it. It is times like these when a fly fisherman can easily score with patterns that match these two creatures. Both anglers and paddlers should plan to spend most of their time on the Baywood float reveling in this four-mile section.

At about the six-mile point, Joyce's Rapid looms. From well upstream, travelers will hear the roar of Joyce's and also spot a series of huge grayish-white boulders that extend from the river-left shoreline. Tom Maxwell of Independence made an excellent map of this part of the New and he recommends that canoeists run the middle of the rapid in order to miss several large boulders on the left side of the rapid, one-third of the way down. Maxwell admonishes paddlers to keep to the right of those boulders. I enjoy running Joyce's Rapid, as it clips along at a good pace under normal water level conditions. However, if spring runoff raises the New River, this rapid should be portaged on river left. In any season, Joyce's offers some stunning shots for the shutterbug. The aforementioned river-left boulders provide several perches for photographers.

Some excellent fishing exists immediately below Joyce's for about a quarter mile. The rest of the trip, though, offers limited fishing, floating, and photographic opportunities. The river bottom becomes very sandy and gravelly and the water is less than a foot deep in many places. Late summer floaters may have to spend time dragging their craft. Tragically, the upper New River in North Carolina and Virginia has suffered severe runoff problems from agricultural concerns, and this section is prime evidence of that fact. Summer homes and trailers line the river-left side, so scenic vistas are limited. Near the eight-mile point, Elk Creek enters on river left providing a landmark as does a river-right island. Paddle quickly through this section to the river-left take-out. The Baywood float is one of startling contrasts from marvelous solitude to a silted-in river, but the trip is still very much worth taking.

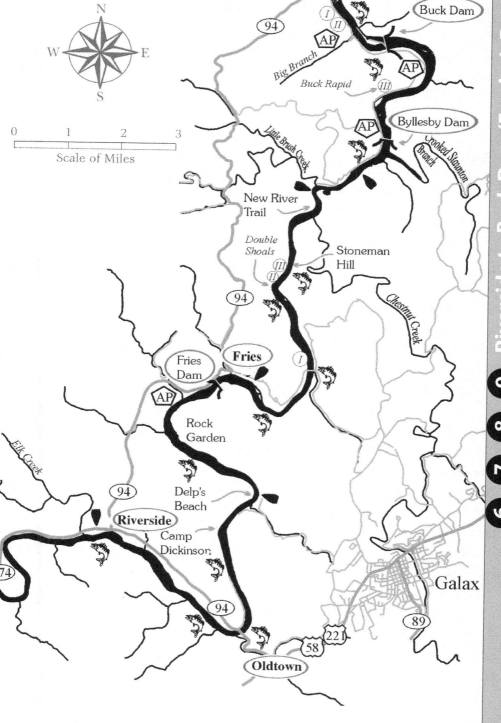

9

6 7 8 9

⑥ Riverside to Oldtown

TRIP: Riverside to Oldtown in Grayson County

USGS QUADS: Brierpatch Mountain and Galax

DISTANCE: Six miles

MAP: Page 86

RAPIDS: Riffles

ACCESS: At Riverside, the river-left put-in is near the intersection of Routes 274 and 94. The ramp is gravel, and parking spaces are numerous. At Oldtown, the take-out is on river right, off Route 641. The ramp is gravel, and parking spaces are numerous.

The Riverside junket is an easy half-day float for anglers and a pleasant three-hour run for paddlers. The major drawback is that long stretches of very shallow water exist. Sedimentation is a major problem on this part of the New River.

Some of the best fishing and sightseeing occurs at the beginning of this trip. Right out from the launch site, a series of deep-water riffles begins; and the fishing can be outstanding. On one August float, three fellow float fishermen and I lingered within sight of the put-in for nearly an hour as the smallmouths constantly hammered our topwater offerings. This is a marvelous locale for long rodders to toss Sneaky Pete poppers, hair bugs, and grasshopper patterns and for spin fishermen to fling Heddon Tiny Torpedos, Phillips Crippled Killers, and Rebel Pop'Rs to the many current breaks behind midstream rocks and ledges. Most of this rock cover lies in water under five feet, so wade fishermen, if they are careful and if they have donned life jackets, can experience gratifying action near the launch site. Another plus for this section is that several small bluffs line the river-right side and offer photographic opportunities. Also note that two major islands lie near the river-left shoreline and are popular spots for camping and shore lunches. Please be sure to leave these islands free of litter and to even pick up trash that others may have left behind.

The riffle/pool habitat that occurs at the beginning of this float continues, in fact, over most of the first two miles of the Riverside getaway. For much of these two miles, the river-right shoreline is heavily wooded and the river-left shoreline is a mixture of agricultural land and scattered trailers. In many places, Route 94 is also visible from the latter shoreline. An outstanding photographic opportunity also appears between the one and two-mile points as a gorgeous rock outcropping dominates the river-right shore. Paddle just downstream from this bluff and shoot upstream to capture a curve in the river. The goal here is to take advantage of the classic photographic rule of thirds. For this particular shot, the photo should consist of roughly equal portions of bluff, curving river, and sky.

Unfortunately, soon after this bluff, the sedimentation problem on the upper river rears its ugly head. Well-known river guide Shawn Hash of Tangent Outfitters once told me that this part of the New could be described as being "long stretches of oasis followed by long stretches of desert." Some of this "desert" now comes into existence as the river is barely a foot deep in many places until the Route 94 Bridge appears between the three and four-mile points. The water is often so shallow that if the summer has been dry, the Riverside float may not be feasible by late August or September.

Fortunately, the shallow, sandy water ends a hundred yards or so above the Route 94 Bridge as a series of boulders and ledges create riffles and some depth. This is another wonderful place to take pictures as the combination of rocky habitat in the foreground and of the bridge in the background creates pleasing images. Another photo possibility occurs just downstream from the bridge as another series of ledges, boulders, and riffles characterize the river.

Virginia Game Department biologists Bill Kittrell and John Copeland sampling the New below Riverside.

The area just upstream from the bridge and for several hundred yards below has just enough current to make Clouser minnows, streamers, grubs, and crankbaits good choices for fly and spin fishermen. This is also a good section for wade fishermen to make their way down from the Route 94 Bridge and enjoy fine sport.

Just after the four-mile point, a series of shallow water ledges dominate the river for several hundred yards. These areas don't hold smallmouths in the summer and early fall, but they are superior places to find fish in the spring during the pre-spawn and spawning periods. A number of gravel flats also characterize this section and are preferred places for smallmouths, rock bass, and redbreast sunfish to reproduce. At no other time of the year is it more important for anglers to release the fish they catch, for a spawning female of one of these three species easily carries several thousand eggs. But good habitat often does not endure long on the upper river, and the siltation problem continues for well over a half mile. Paddle through this section as quickly as possible and pray that the government will one day require farmers, cattle rearers, and landowners to show more respect for the New.

Just before the five-mile point, a series of four islands split the river. Paddle to the left of these islands to capture the best current and experience the best fishing. The river-left shoreline is characterized by sycamores and the occasional willow and is in full or partial shade for much of the day. The water is often quite deep along this bank and fly fishermen will enjoy success with weighted nymphs and Woolly Buggers while spin fishermen will want to cast plastic worms and craw worms underneath the tree canopies and to the rock and wood cover that line the bank. Camp Dickinson, a Methodist Church operation, appears along this shoreline toward the end of the island passage.

The last mile of the Riverside journey is very slow, shallow, and sandy. A sand dredging business formerly operated along the river-right shoreline and the rusted remains of this company are a major eyesore. Sand dredging operations have both pros and cons. They do remove sedimentation from the river and create deeper water for fish and other aquatic creatures. But they also often destroy riparian zones and cause run-off problems themselves. Not long after you pass the deserted sand company, the river-right take-out comes into view. A strange looking "riffle" can be seen just downstream from this access point. More information about that riffle is in the next chapter.

7 Oldtown to Fries Dam

TRIP: Oldtown to Fries in Grayson County

USGS QUAD: Galax and Brierpatch Mountain

DISTANCE: Two and a half miles

MAP: Page 86

RAPIDS: One Class I and riffles

ACCESS: At Oldtown, the put-in is on river right, off Route 641. The ramp is gravel, and parking spaces are numerous. At Fries, the take-out is a roadside pull-off from Route 94. Parking spaces are extremely limited. The river-left take-out requires that boaters haul their craft up the river bank, through an overgrown field, and up a steep incline to Route 94.

In one way, the Oldtown float can be looked upon as a pleasant, brief, one or two hour getaway for anglers and paddlers. But it also can probably be considered the worst float on the entire New River. The short length, the long one-mile rock garden and riffle section, and some stunning bluffs recommend this section; but pollution, siltation problems in the rock garden, and the worst take-out on the North Carolina and Virginia section of the New are significant negatives.

The pollution enters the river directly below the river-right put-in. What first appears to be a rather unusual "riffle" turns out to be a pipe that extends from the river-right shoreline. At numerous places, this pipe shoots a smelly, grayish effluent into the river, and the disagreeable color and odor continue to assault the river and your senses for several hundred yards downstream. This general area is known as Delp's Beach and primitive camping is available, although I certainly would not want to spend a night there.

The first mile or so of the Oldtown excursion has sections of very deep water, but the bottom cover is limited and silt is a problem. The right shoreline is mostly wooded, with an occasional home while agriculture and pastures dominate the left side. The most pleasurable portion for both float fishermen and paddlers is a mile-long rock garden and riffle zone (with an easy Class I rapid), which comes next. Outdoor enthusiasts will want to linger in this section for a long time as the smallmouth bass fishing is excellent with the many drop-offs and ledges, the paddling is pleasurable with much fun maneuvering between and around boulders, and the picture-taking is grand with all of the rocky backdrops. I have caught smallmouths up to eighteen inches from this section and have espied numerous bigger smallmouths. This is an extremely popular place for wade fishermen as the water is less than four feet deep in many places. Many small islands dot this section and create some excellent wildlife habitat.

The last half mile of this float is really nothing more than the pool above Fries Dam, a forty-foot structure that once was the power source for a textile mill. This part of the Oldtown float offers better fishing for large-mouth bass than smallmouths. Some enticing rock and wood cover lies along an outside bend on river left and results in some angling opportunities, mostly in the spring. A stunning rock bluff rises above the river-right shore-line and offers an outstanding photo opportunity. At about the time the bluff comes into view, look downstream and notice the blue barrels strung across the river. Soon, warning signs for the dam can be glimpsed and boaters will see signs ordering them to take out on the river-left bank. This is a character building exercise as there is no formal take-out and the grassy bank can be slippery. In the summer, boaters will then

Guide Mike Smith of Willis admiring a jumbo New River smallmouth taken on the Oldtown float.

have to make their way through an overgrown field and up a steep foot trail to reach their vehicles. The Oldtown float does have several things to recommend it, but overall, the negatives outweigh the positives.

8 Fries to Byllesby Reservoir

TRIP: Fries to Byllesby Reservoir in Grayson and Carroll counties

USGS QUADS: Galax and Austinville

DISTANCE: Seven miles

MAP: Page 86

RAPIDS: Class II-III Double Shoals and several Class Is and riffles

ACCESS: At Fries, the put-in is on river left, approximately half a mile below Fries Dam, off Route 94 at Riverside Park. The ramp is gravel, and parking spaces are numerous in the gravel lot. The take-out is approximately one mile above Byllesby Dam. The concrete ramp is on river right at the end of Route 739. Parking places are numerous in the gravel lot.

Seldom do sections of trips on the New or any river have as much contrast as the sections on the Fries excursion. Basically, this junket should be divided into three very different sections and approached in that manner. If you decide to run the entire trip as a whole, I recommend that you and your boat mate be expert canoeists. Double Shoals Rapid dominates the midsection of this float and endures in one form or another for well over a mile. In high water, sections of Double Shoals contain Class III rapids and even at normal summer levels, Double Shoals flaunts strong Class IIs. Even intermediate paddlers may find the intensity and duration of this rapid overly challenging. Canoeists should allot four hours for the trip as a whole and anglers should plan for a full day on the water.

"The Double Shoals section is a very impressive stretch of water," said guide Ben Lucas of Rock On Charters. "The habitat there is some of the best on the New, especially the ledges and steady current. The current breaks and eddies all add to the high quality. Really, this is what classic smallmouth habitat looks like."

Eric Cockerham of Mount Airy, North Carolina, frequently runs this junket.

"Fishermen should never run this trip in a canoe," he said. "Please use either a kayak or a raft-like boat, as even a drift boat might not have enough clearance to float this section in the summer. The smallmouth fishing is great on the Fries float, but it is also the most dangerous trip to take above Claytor Lake. Double Shoals is the reason why this trip is so dangerous. That rapid just has too many boulders, that you can't see, right under the surface. And that's true at all water levels and all seasons.

"Double Shoals has so many rapids and so many drops and boulders that sometimes when I take this float I feel like a bumper car in an amusement park ride. But the smallmouth bass fishing can be outstanding there."

The float begins innocently enough within the town limits of Fries. Fries is a fascinating small town to drive through with its row houses and mom-and-pop stores and restaurants. For much of the twentieth century, Fries was a typical Southern mill town, which was why a dam was built there. But when the mill ownership closed up shop and left town, the town experienced hard economic times, which continue today. I believe Fries would be a great place to have a canoe livery or a sporting goods store that dealt at least in part with river running. There are certainly enough quality float trips above and below this community. Warm-weather wade fishermen can enjoy some pleasing fishing within sight of the ramp and Fries Dam. Some waders, in fact, like to carefully pick their way upstream and work the riffles and small pools that are found all the way to the dam. Although I have made this comment before, it bears repeating. I always wear a lifejacket on the New and other streams while I am wading, and I strongly recommend that you do, too. Even though the tailwater section of this area is relatively mild much of the time, dangerous undertows are also present, and water levels can rise unexpectedly.

On one float through this section, fellow angler Lou Giusto of Woodstock and I caught several good-quality smallmouths along the river-right shoreline near the put-in. Giusto tossed a soft plastic jerkbait behind the current breaks while I employed a buzzbait under the overhanging tree limbs. This is a super place to begin the trip as trees and rock bluffs characterize the bank while homes and backyards dominate the opposite side. Though we worked the right shoreline because shade still covered that bank, good habitat can be found from shoreline to shoreline throughout much of the first half mile of this float. Next, you will come to a shallow, sandy section that offers limited fishing potential but very pleasurable floating. During warm weather jaunts, this area is a fine place to do some bird watching and take photos. Red-eyed vireos dwell in great numbers along the wooded river-right shore while song sparrows can be heard frequently on the opposite bank.

The next section is very long and straight as the New leaves Fries behind. Cornfields lie along river left, and the river-right hillsides are heavily wooded. Occasional small riffles and midstream boulders appear as you drift by. Route

606 parallels the left shoreline, and cars can be heard from time to time. The first section of this float concludes when Route 606 crosses the river; this area is further marked by the sandy island immediately upstream from the bridge. An informal take-out exists on river right below the bridge. Again, if you are not an expert canoeist, I recommend debarking here. On the aforementioned trip with Lou Giusto, we were in his raft. I consider my wife Elaine and myself capable intermediate canoeists, but we would not have attempted to travel further in our boat.

The second section of the Fries float now begins and the first half mile or so of it consists of very slow moving water and extremely scenic views on both sides. Several old barns lie along river left, and these are gorgeous structures to photograph. A Class I ledge then appears and offers some very enticing fishing. Long rodders should toss damsel and dragonfly patterns both above and below this area as these two winged predators are often out in force. Spin fishermen can find success with all manner of topwaters. Numerous rocks then stud the river for several hundred yards until another Class I ledge comes into view. A rock garden also lies below this ledge. It was here on one trip that I experienced some outstanding surface action in the middle of a June day. Using Heddon Tiny Torpedos and Rapala Skitter Pops, I caught a number of smallmouths in the two-pound range. I don't know why the middle of the day topwater bite can be so good on many rivers; perhaps it is because various aquatic hatches take place then. But this strong surface feeding period is something I have witnessed many times on many streams during the noon hour.

Double Shoals Rapids then comes into view. The river drops some forty feet over the course of this rapid, which can be divided into two sections. Some strong Class IIs, which become Class IIIs during high water, pop up repeatedly and unexpectedly. They often require deft maneuvering, and portaging is difficult given the steep, heavily wooded banks on both sides. Over halfway through this section of Double Shoals, you will spot a river-right island and a rock bluff. The island is a fine place to take a break and calm your nerves. Next comes a mild riffle section, making unassuming floaters believe that they have left Double Shoals behind. Actually, while the most intense part of Double Shoals is its upper part, the lower level is quite daunting, as well.

Some very tricky drops exist there, and hydraulics are present in a number of places. The smallmouth fishing, though, can be tremendous. On Giusto's and my trip, he remarked that the fish through here acted as if they had never

The view downstream from Fries Dam.

seen a lure. Indeed, no hook marks existed on the smallies we caught, making his observation very likely to be true. It was also in this section that I caught one of my biggest smallmouth bass ever. I was casting a Skitter Pop to some rocky backwaters on river left when a resounding splash covered up my lure. I immediately knew that I had a jumbo brown bass on, but at that same moment the strong current carried us through a rapid. The smallmouth seized that moment to dash under a ledge and as Giusto's raft headed downstream, I could feel the smallmouth rubbing my line against the bottom of the ledge—a sure sign that I would soon lose the fish and lure. I yelled for Lou to stop the raft, and he expertly maneuvered the craft across the current and to the bank, where I hopped out. Splashing my way across the shallows as I headed upstream for the ledge, and the bass underneath, I was chagrined to see that the bass had looped the line around the ledge and was now charging furiously downstream. In short, the bass and I were only a few yards apart, but there was some forty yards of line between the fish and me. I finally extricated the line from the upstream ledge, only to find that the brown bass, which now had leaped four times and displayed some amazing girth, had swum even further downstream and entangled the line in an overhanging silver maple. I finally removed the line from the maple; the smallie jumped yet again, and then scooted under yet another ledge. Like most anglers, I have fought and lost big bass many times before, but this battle had gone on so long and I was so exhausted that I was now quite ready to end the affair, one way or another. I reached under the ledge in an attempt to land the smallmouth, but the fish made one last run. Fortunately, Lou was ready with his net and he corralled the bass. After we took a few quick photos, Lou measured the smallmouth—all twenty-one and three-fourths inches. Releasing the trophy, I watched it return to the same lie where I had caught it and again take up a feeding position. Obviously, I was much more tired than that fish was.

And this was not the only time I have seen trophy smallmouth caught from Double Shoals. On an excursion with guides Ken Trail and Ben Lucas, Ken landed a smallie that was in the four-pound range. Yes, Double Shoals can be hard to fish at times and always offers the potential for a dangerous mishap, but it is true big smallie water.

Through the lower section of Double Shoals, Stoneman Hill is the most recognizable shoreline feature as it presents an imposing sight on river right. Finally, the rapids and rock gardens come to an end as riffles and rocks take their place. You will then note a midstream island, a railroad bridge, and Chestnut Creek entering on river right. The third section of the Fries float now begins and offers little for the float fisherman. The river-right bank is very pretty with white pines, Canada hemlocks, and Catawba rhododendron characterizing the surroundings. Little Brush Creek and the New River Trail can be seen on river left. There is even a very picturesque spot where a bridge crosses Little Brush, and a few islands scattered about also add charm. But the backwaters of Byllesby Dam make this a very uninspiring section to paddle. Plan to spend forty-five minutes or so dipping a paddle until you come to the river-right take-out about one mile above Byllesby Dam. On summer days, expect to see power boaters and water skiers here. These signs of civilization contrast sharply with the wild, untamed nature of the New just upstream.

9 Byllesby Dam to Buck Dam

TRIP: From below Byllesby Dam to above Buck Dam in Carroll County

USGS QUAD: Austinville

DISTANCE: Two and a half miles

RAPIDS: Class III Buck Rapid and riffles

MAP: Page 86

ACCESS: River-left put-in is a dirt path immediately below Byllesby Dam. That path is off a gravel road, Route 737, which is off Route 602 via Route 94. Parking consists of roadside pull-offs. The river-left take-out is off Route 737 immediately above Byllesby Dam. Boats must be hauled up a dirt incline of about five yards. Parking is limited above Buck Dam.

At first glance, one might wonder why bother with such a short float sandwiched between two small power dams—relics of a time when the conventional wisdom was that damming rivers was good for the prosperity of an area. Actually, I strongly believe now that these two dams and the one at Fries have kept what could have become a world-class whitewater rafting, kayaking, and canoeing industry from developing in the area. In short, these three dams have hurt the economy of the area and have kept jobs away. In the future, the demand for outdoor recreation will only increase and more and more people will want to participate in various water sports. And these three dams will sit astride the New River as monuments to the ignorance of a bygone era.

My political opinions aside, the Byllesby float does have much to offer if you are looking for a pleasant afternoon junket. Canoeists can easily complete this getaway in less than two hours and fishermen can work the best places in about three hours. Upon debarking from a dirt path below Byllesby Dam, you will spot several islands. Take the main channel down the middle of the river. For most of the year, the water is quite shallow through here and small ledges characterize the river. Wade fishermen may want to check out these ledges but should also know that water levels below the dam can rise quickly and unexpectedly. The New River Trail runs along river left; expect to see hikers and horseback riders meandering along. Less than a mile into this float, the only major riffle appears and offers some high-quality fishing. This is a fine section for the fly fisherman who favors topwater patterns. The water is only a few feet deep in many places, and the riffle area teems with aggressive smallmouths.

Next, you will spot a power line crossing the river and hear the sounds of a major drop in the streambed: the Class III Buck Rapids. Tom Maxwell, a surveyor from Independence, accompanied me on my initial voyage down this section. We took one look at the precipitous drop present at Buck Rapids and immediately agreed to portage. Buck Rapids is a very technical ledge with some impressive, and dangerous, boulders at its center. A small island lies to the left of the center of the rapid, and that's where Maxwell and I portaged and where I recommend you do the same unless you are an expert canoeist. The conventional wisdom is that this rapid is best run on the center or left; but, again, my conventional wisdom is to portage. The riffle areas immediately above and below Buck Rapids are extremely popular places for wade fishermen and sunbathers since a campground exists nearby. And the hillsides on both sides of the river are very beautiful as the trail on the left, and the rock formations, hemlocks, and rhododendron on the right add charm.

After you leave Buck Rapids behind, you will want to paddle quickly through the pool above Buck Dam. Heavy siltation has occurred here, so much so that a muck island, now covered with cattails and willows, has grown on river left over the past half century or so. Maxwell said the island did not exist when he was growing up in the area during the 1950s. Just above the dam, you will need to paddle beyond the tip of that island and maneuver left to reach a river-left dirt bank that serves as the take-out.

Portaging the Class III Buck Rapid is often wise.

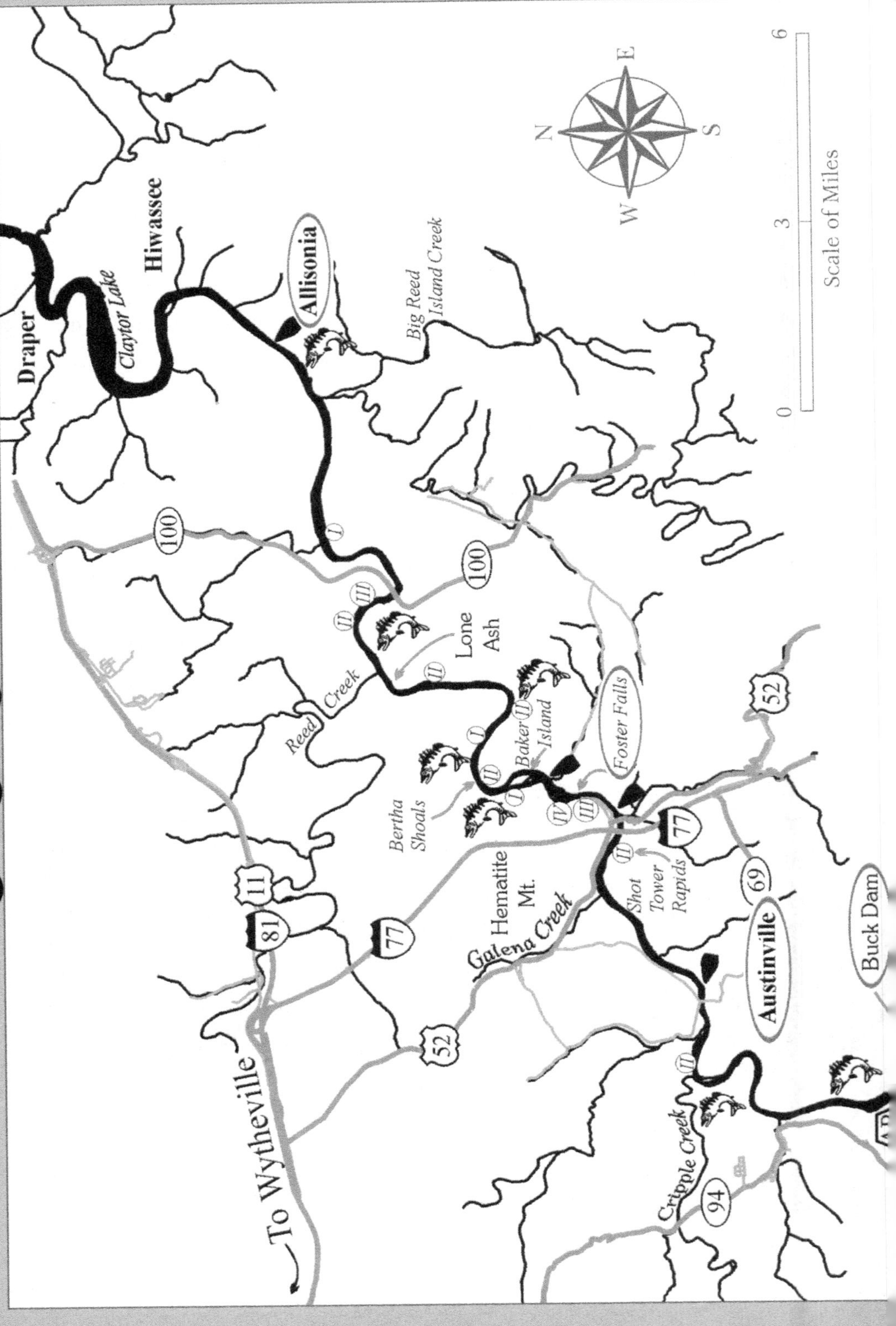

Draper

Hiwassee

Claytor Lake

Allisonia

Big Reed Island Creek

N E S W

Scale of Miles

0 3 6

100

100

I

III
II

Lone Ash

Reed Creek

Baker Island

I

II

Foster Falls

Bertha Shoals

II
I
II
IV
III

52

77

Shot Tower Rapids

II

69

Hematite Mt.

Galena Creek

81

111

77

52

To Wytheville

Austinville

Buck Dam

II

Cripple Creek

94

10 11 12

⑩ Buck Dam to Austinville

TRIP: Fowler's Ferry (Buck Dam) to Austinville in Carroll and Wythe counties

USGS QUAD: Austinville

DISTANCE: Seven and a half miles

MAP: Page 98

RAPIDS: Class Is and several Class IIs

ACCESS: Put-in is off an impassable Route 658, below Buck Dam. Route 658 via Route 94 (Ivanhoe Road). A gravel parking lot exists there and a path leads to the river. Take-out is at a river-right concrete ramp just past the Route 636 Bridge at Austinville. A large paved parking lot exists.

Although the mileage between Fowler's Ferry, which basically means below Buck Dam, and Austinville is listed as seven and a half miles, in reality paddlers will only be able to paddle about six miles of the trip. That is because there is no access point below the dam for well over a mile. A river-right dirt road runs along a cliff above the section, but to access the river, one would have to drag her craft down a precipitous hillside and across some heath-like bottomland to reach the river. That is too bad because the New is simply gorgeous above the actual roadside put-in. Boulders stud the river in numerous places and Class I to II rapids beckon the float fisherman and canoeist. That call will have to go unanswered, however, since the river flows too swiftly for an outdoorsman to paddle upstream for any appreciable distance. One possible way to at least reach the river is to walk along Route 639 until you come to Big Branch, which enters the New on river left. Wade fishermen can then follow this small creek until they reach the river. Driving to Big Branch is not recommended because the road is so narrow; no place exists to park a vehicle, unless you assume that no one else will drive by. It is possible for paddlers to portage around Buck Dam by following a road between the emergency spillway and the powerhouse. A trail leads from the powerhouse down to a channel below the structure. This portage is about a quarter of a mile.

Once you do access the river, expect to enjoy a gorgeous section of the New River. Float fishermen will find this a long afternoon of angling while canoeists can easily negotiate the section in three hours with stops for picture taking and scenery gazing. Wade fishermen can experience some good-quality sport around the put-in. The first "real" mile of this excursion offers outstanding fishing. The initial major feature is a small island that cleaves the New and creates a riffle on its left side. Take that route and immediately start casting to the river-left shoreline, which is characterized by numerous basketball-sized rocks, overhanging sycamores, and occasional laydowns. On my first visit to this section, which was in May, I was impressed by the numbers of bird species that were singing along this bank. Acadian flycatchers, eastern wood peewees, orchard orioles,

and a host of other avian species competed to see which could best serenade my canoe downstream. This bank is an excellent one for long rodders to cast hair bugs and various terrestrials, while spin fishermen will likely score with Phillips Crippled Killers, Heddon Tiny Torpedoes, and buzzbaits.

The next one-to-two mile section of this float also has much to recommend it. Several rocky points characterize the river-left side while a series of four bluffs define the river-right shoreline. All of these places hold smallmouths and walleyes. Cliff swallows also make their homes

The Buck Dam to Austinville excursion contains a number of scenic views.

in those bluffs. Mike Smith, a guide on the river from Willis, relates that the New has a devoted, and highly secretive, walleye contingent that like to float this section under cover of darkness. As noted earlier, I have generally found walleye fishermen to be the worst liars among the fishing society. Many fishermen hedge, prevaricate, and obfuscate about how and where they are having success. And I include myself and my best fishing buddies among this group. But marble-eye enthusiasts, who relish the tasty fillets of this species, have taken the art of not divulging information to a new level. These individuals often deny that they are even angling for walleyes, let alone that they are experiencing good fortune doing so. I have always believed that they are so secretive about their success because so few Southerners are good at catching this predominantly Northern species.

The next major feature is what appears to be a manmade ledge that crosses the river. This "ledge" is perfectly straight and spans the stream, creating some good fishing directly above and below it. A small creek enters the New soon after the ledge and a long, deep pool ensues. It was during this section that Brady Sheffer of Roanoke and I once had a close encounter with a hornet's nest that had been constructed along the river-right shoreline. Brady had hurled his plastic lizard into a sycamore and I obligingly offered to remove the bait. However, when I saw that the lure had come to rest on the same limb that supported the hornet's home, I asked my friend to cut his line and leave the area. We then engaged in one of those conversations that anglers can only have on rivers, about the relative pain that can be inflicted by hornets, wasps, honeybees, and a host of other stinging creatures and whether a lure is worth that pain. I said no bait was, but it was not my lizard that was dangling from a tree. Sheffer decided to brave the wrath of the hornets and luckily retrieved his lure without being stung.

Near the end of the trip, a railroad bridge crosses the river, and this area is simply one of the most gorgeous on the float. Whenever I see a bridge spanning a river, I like to leave my canoe and have my companion paddle around in the vicinity of it. The framing of the water, canoe, bridge, and sky make for fabulous photographs. The last major feature is a Class II rapid that runs all the way across the New. The safest path is on far river left and is the side I recommend boaters take. However, thrill seekers and expert canoeists may want to tempt fate and try to make their way through one of the slots on far river right. Beware: this rapid can turn into a Class III during high water conditions. Another note of caution must be sounded for the riffle below this rapid. Some thirty-five steel bars are imbedded in the stream bottom, remnants of a previous structure. During low water conditions especially, these bars can be a navigation hazard. The Fowler's Ferry float concludes at the Route 636 Bridge; the takeout is under this structure on river right. Despite river runners not being able to realistically float all of this section, it still is a very worthwhile journey.

11 Austinville to Jackson Ferry

TRIP: Austinville to Jackson Ferry (Fosters Falls) in Wythe County

USGS QUADS: Austinville, Max Meadow, and Fosters Falls

DISTANCE: Three and a half miles

MAP: Page 98

RAPIDS: Class II Shot Tower Rapid and riffles

ACCESS: Put-in is at a river-right concrete ramp just past the Route 636 Bridge near Austinville. A large paved parking lot exists. The take-out is at a river-right concrete ramp immediately above Fosters Falls, a Class III-IV rapid. The ramp is in the New River Trail State Park off Route 608. A large gravel parking lot exists nearby.

Of all the float trips possible on the New in North Carolina, Virginia, and West Virginia, I rate this one as the worst for the fisherman. If you are a paddler who seeks adventure and rip-roaring rapids, seek both elsewhere. But if you are a novice paddler who wants to experience a lazy afternoon and some enchanting country streamsides, then the Austinville getaway is for you. Since there are so few places to fish and since the water flows so slowly along, both the float fisherman and canoeist should be able to undergo this trip in about four hours. The only place that could cause a paddler trouble is the Class II Shot Tower Rapids, and plenty of places exist where you can either avoid the heart of this rapid or portage it on river right.

After you put-in below the Route 636 Bridge, you will be greeted by some beautiful wooded banks on both sides of the river intermixed with scattered houses on river left. Route 619 flows along much of the river-left bank and provides bank fishermen with access, provided they receive permission to cross private land. The Austinville junket continues like this for several miles until you reach the Class II Shot Tower Rapids. These rapids are named for the nearby Shot Tower, which businessman Tom Jackson constructed in the early 1800s. The tower stands 75 feet tall and was used to manufacture shot pellets for the young United States and later briefly for the South during the Civil War. Below the base of the tower, a shaft extends another 75 feet. A kettle existed at the top of the tower and dropped hot lead 150 feet to a large water-filled kettle at the bottom of the shaft. At the time, the belief was that the long fall was needed in order for the shot to properly mold. The tower's rock walls, which are 2½ feet thick, were thought necessary to keep the interior at a constant, cool temperature. Today, the Shot Tower is part of the New River Trail State Park.

The riffles immediately above and below Shot Tower Rapids, a rocky river-right bank below the rapid, and the heart of the rapids themselves are really the only places that the smallmouth bass enthusiast will want to angle on this trip. The most challenging part of Shot Tower is on far river left at the end of this some one-hundred-yard-long rapid. This is where a boulder studs the river and causes a hydraulic. Tom Maxwell, who is an expert on this section of the New and has created several maps covering the confluence to Claytor Lake,

The end of Foster Falls, shown here, is runnable, but the upstream side of it definitely is not.

says that walleye anglers like the slow water above and below Shot Tower Rapids, especially in the spring. I noted earlier that these rapids provide the only hazard on the Austinville float, but that even novice floaters should be able to negotiate Shot Tower successfully. On a trip through here with Maxwell, we watched as a canoe overturned, dumping its two inhabitants. We later talked to them, and their biggest concern was that they had lost their supply of alcohol. Drinking alcohol and paddling a river definitely do not mix; that intoxicated twosome was lucky that they did not suffer serious injury.

After you pass through Shot Tower Rapids, you will spot several landmarks; in succession Interstate 77 and Route 52 cross the river, and an informal take-out exists on river right under the Route 52 Bridge. Between these two bridges, you should be able to see the Shot Tower on river right. A twenty-minute paddle later, you will spot a river-right bluff, a power line, the remains of a stone railroad abutment, and a large metal cylinder that lies right of center. These are all clues that you are about to arrive at the river-right take-out immediately above Foster Falls.

12 Jackson Ferry to Allisonia

TRIP: Jackson Ferry (Foster Falls) to Allisonia in Wythe and Pulaski counties

USGS QUADS: Foster Falls and Hiwassee

DISTANCE: Thirteen and a half miles

MAP: Page 98

RAPIDS: Class III-IV Foster Falls, a three-hundred-yard long rapid; numerous Class Is and IIs and riffles

ACCESS: A river-right concrete ramp exists below Foster Falls in the New River Trail State Park off Route 608. A large gravel parking lot exists nearby. The take-out is on river right at a concrete ramp off Route 693. Parking spaces are numerous.

Before beginning the Jackson Ferry (Foster Falls) trip, you may be interested in some history of the area. The town of Foster Falls, now the site of just a few homes, a church, and post office, was once a focal point for the New River Valley's iron production. The community boasted the Foster Falls Furnace, a hotel, railroad station, distillery, and various mills. More than a hundred company-owned homes were constructed by the iron industry. As often happens in river towns, a flood destroyed the furnace in 1914, changing the local economy forever. Today, outdoor enthusiasts can access the New River Trail from the Foster Falls' put-in. Millrace Campground also exists on the site.

I have taken this trip a number of times in various seasons and on various excursions have targeted smallies, walleyes, and muskies. Captain Forest Pressnell, who operates New River Charter and concentrates on taking clients on the lower half of the upper New in Virginia, guides for all three of the aforementioned game fish. Equally adept with both spinning and fly tackle, Forest also has assisted the Virginia Game Department with its muskie and walleye programs. By far, the best marble-eye sport is on the New above Claytor.

"Typical small mouth raft float trips are 12.5 or 7 miles depending on the current flow of the river with the smallmouth 'season' running April through October," said Pressnell. "Walleye trips are run to target the spawning fish in February and March. Muskie fishing is great year round."

Forest says that the Foster Falls float is one of the premier ones on the New and guide Ken Trail of Rock On Charters agrees.

"This is a big time bass float with big time bass action," said Ken. "And this trip also offers big time walleye action in the spring. I think one of the reason this float is so exceptional is the ledge structure. Below lots of those ledges are rapids and below those rapids are boulder filled runs. Places like those hide trophy smallmouths all year long."

Trail says anglers can work jig and pigs through this type of water as well as jumbo spinnerbaits, but topwater action can be stupendous during the summer.

"This trip has winter holes, spring holes, summer holes, and fall holes," said Trail. "You can't go wrong coming here."

The Jackson Ferry junket is definitely a long day for the float fisherman; little time is available for dawdling. Canoeists should plan on six to seven hours. However, even though this trip is extremely long, it is one of the premier treks on the entire New River for fishermen, canoeists, bird watchers, and photographers. Although I listed the Class III-IV Foster Falls in the gray box at the start of this chapter, the actual put-in is just below the rapid on river right. Unless you are an expert canoeist or a kayaker or rafter, I do not recommend running Foster Falls. Immediately after you debark from the put-in, you will see a power line and the approximately half-mile-long Baker Island. Take the right passage for the most water and the best fishing. Baker Island is a gorgeous place and hosts numerous shorebirds, warblers, and herons. Part way through the passage, a Class I-II rapid forms. Numerous passageways exist, but boulders also stud this rapid depending on water levels. Portage this rapid along the island, especially if the New is running high and muddy. State fisheries biologist George Palmer reports that walleyes thrive in this area, and the shade cast by the heavily wooded island and the river-right bank make this a smallmouth hot spot throughout even the steamiest summer day. At the end of Baker Island, another power line crosses the river and a Class II ledge forms; run this one in the slot on far river left.

The next major feature is the infamous Bertha Shoals, which forms in an extended river-left bend. In short, this is one of the most bizarre rapids I have encountered on any river. A ledge runs down from the river-left bluff and across the river, creating a wicked non-stop series of sharply pointed outcroppings. The current flows very swiftly above and below those outcroppings, and immediately below them is another ledge and a sharp drop in the stream bottom. Indeed, a series of ledges exist below this first outcropping, creating a very challenging Class II. On my first visit to Bertha, I finally gave up looking for chutes and portaged on river right. The fishing can be phenomenal in this area, but many boaters have also been caught by the fiercely flowing current and capsized when trying to navigate Bertha's ledges. After a long pool with good current, Bertha continues presenting stunning scenery, especially when matched with the heavily wooded shorelines. This is an extremely photogenic setting, until another power line crosses the New, basically ending the Bertha Shoals area. Even though the Jackson Ferry trip is a long one, it is hard not to linger here.

"Bertha is one of the most intriguing rapids I've ever seen on the New," said James River guide Richard Furman. "The river makes a hard bend and the ledges dissect that bend in multiple places creating the worst cross currents I know of. If the water is running at even moderate levels, and you overturn in those ledges, you are in serious trouble. It's a beautiful place and very unique, but it is also very dangerous. There's good fishing on the back sides of those ledges, but, again, if you get involved with your fishing and don't watch what you are doing, you could be in trouble. This is just not a good place for a novice paddler."

I would add that this rapid becomes worse the higher it becomes. I have charged through Bertha in the summer and also in late winter when the water was higher. The rapid definitely has more force in higher water. Some rapids smooth out in higher water; this one does not.

After the river-left bend concludes, a Class I-II is immediately followed by another Class II. During high water, portage on river left. Once again, this section of the New offers superlative fishing, especially if you enjoy employing swiftly moving offerings such as streamers, grubs, and buzzbaits. A long straight stretch then ensues, but the current clips along at a good pace, creating well-aerated water, fine fishing, and more appealing scenery. The New River Trail meanders along the river-right bank and occasionally you can spot horseback riders, bikers, and hikers. An approximately 100-yard-long Class II rapid then looms and forms a very precipitous drop. Although the streambed does decline noticeably here, this is not an overly difficult rapid to negotiate. Portage it on river left or run it on the left, as well.

The river once again slows and passes some fields on river left and heavily wooded hillsides on the right. I cannot adequately describe how beautiful the New is not only through this section of the Jackson Ferry float but throughout the entire getaway. The bird watching alone is phenomenal but so are the fishing, canoeing, and picture taking. On one trip, I watched a pair of red-tailed hawks teaching their offspring how to soar and hunt while an osprey "fished" the river. Wood thrushes lent their lilting flute-like songs to the proceedings and yellow-throated vireos, yellow-breasted chats, black-and-white warblers, and a host of other species joined in. On that same trip, I landed a three-pound smallmouth, shot numerous pictures , and had my canoeing ability tested. Who can ask for more from a river?

The Jackson Ferry to Allisonia trek provides splendid solitude and superb smallmouth sport.

After Reed Creek commingles with the New on river left, be prepared for some satisfying fishing for the next several miles. Although a series of large rocks are present below the confluence, the great fishing actually begins several hundred yards downstream in the area above Carter Island. A series of three riffles also make up this part of the float, and each riffle seems to offer progressively better fishing and deeper water. Fine fishing also occurs immediately above Carter Island, and some gray bluffs line the river-left shoreline and the heavily wooded forest continues unabated on river right. I should say what remains of Carter Island; the left side of the island is heavily silted, making this island really a part of that bank now. The next major feature is a Class II-III rapid that offers no clear pathway through its maze of basketball-sized and larger rocks. I recommend portaging this rapid on river left. A nice pool forms below this rapid and is a great place to work crayfish patterns, tube baits, and Carolina-rigged lizards and grubs. Soon you will spot the Route 100 Bridge and will note that the river narrows noticeably before once again broadening after you pass under the bridge. The next several miles of the New provide fine action for muskies and walleyes as the river flows very slowly and the water is quite deep. Smallmouth fans, however, will want to quickly paddle through this section. Scattered fields and houses characterize the river-left shoreline, and wooded hillsides and occasional bluffs dominate the right bank. One particularly interesting bluff is very narrow and pointed. Be sure to take pictures of these bluffs and the pastoral vistas.

The superlative smallmouth fishing then returns. Water willow and numerous ledges line the river-left bank especially and the topwater action can be excellent. Indeed, the smallmouth habitat throughout the next few miles is marvelous. Scattered, water willow covered islets are everywhere as are eddies, backwaters, and runs. The super fishing continues as Swan Branch enters on river left and a series of Class I rapids dot the New. For me, the temptation is to spend several hours in this section alone, but this trip as a whole is so long that to do so would be unwise. A power line then crosses the river and riffles, deep-water ledges, and more water willow beds ensue. The river-right bank is also quite rock-strewn in places. This part of the New is known as Reed Junction.

For the rest of the trip, I rate the fishing potential merely as good instead of outstanding. Reed Island Creek enters on river right and you can see a bridge over the creek that is part of the New River Trail. A few minutes more of paddling will bring you to a cable that stretches across the river. You can also see the Allisonia water level gauge on river left. All that is left of the Jackson Ferry trip is a series of riffles and then a twenty-minute or so paddle to the take-out on river right. The backwaters of Claytor Lake slow the river and in effect temporarily end your exploration of the New. But my, what a trip Jackson Ferry has been!

Scale of Miles

0   3   6

Ripplemead

AP

460

Pembroke

Pearisburg

Horshoe Bend

460

N

W   E

S

Pembroke Rapid

II

II

II

Eggleston

AP

II

Big Walker Creek

Goodwins Ferry

I II

I II

AP

IV

III

McCoy Falls (Big Falls)

Norris Run

Tom's Creek

Whitethorne

Longshop

Parrott

Radford Arsenal

Belspring

Pepper's Ferry Bridge

III

114

Radford Arsenal Rapid

II

I

Fairlawn

II

I

11

11

Dublin

Radford

177

81

I II

81

Little River

Claytor Lake Dam

13 Claytor Lake Dam to Bissett Park

TRIP: Claytor Lake Dam to Bissett Park

DISTANCE: Five miles

MAP: Page 110

COUNTIES: Pulaski and Montgomery

USGS QUADS: Radford South and Radford North

RAPIDS: A Class II and I, a number of riffles

ACCESS: The river-right put-in, which is five hundred or so yards below Claytor Lake Dam, is off Route 605, via Route 232, which is off Interstate 81. The ramp is concrete, and parking spaces are numerous in a gravel lot. The river right take-out at Bissett Park is a concrete ramp within a spacious paved parking lot. The park is located right after where Route 232 passes the Route 11 Bridge in Radford. Once inside the park, follow New River Drive to the access point.

One of the most spectacular days I have ever had on the New was on this section while afloat with guide Britt Stoudenmire, who operates the New River Outdoor Company along with his wife Leigh. Britt taught me how to dead drift poppers that day to catch big smallmouth bass that were hunkered down in the shade along the banks or ensconced in elodea beds.

"This float starts off as a major pool below the dam and then flows into a major set of shallow ledges below the route I-81 Bridge," said Britt. "Off and on ledges dot the entire section to Bisset Park mixed with shallow riffles and small pools. Not a great section when the water is up because there are very few shore line eddies, and the best fish holding habitat at many times is mid-river."

Float fishermen should allow five hours for this excursion while canoeists should be able to negotiate this section in two hours or so. Fishermen with motorized johnboats prefer to put in below the dam and fish for striped bass, flathead catfish, and largemouth bass. The Little River also enters the New on river right directly below the dam, and this area also attracts anglers. Claytor Lake was created for power generation; thus, water levels can rise quickly. Caution is advised when fishing or wading in the dam area. For smallmouth anglers, this area offers only fair fishing. Some rock cover exists along the river-left shoreline, and a few grass beds dot the river-right bank. Soon you will pass under the Interstate 81 Bridge and spot a small island on your right. Grass beds lie to the right of the island, and a riffle forms in the area, as well. Some fair wood cover, in the form of laydowns, exists downstream from the island and another riffle comes into view, as well. The first point of real interest is a long Class I-II rapid, depending on water levels, that begins about three hundred yards below the Interstate 81 Bridge. This rapid should be run down the center as a number of rocks stud the right side.

There are some important points worth mentioning about the Claytor Lake Dam float. The lack of swift water makes this trip an appealing one to undertake in the spring when the rest of the New can be running high.

Britt Stoudenmire notes that this trip is often underrated because of the lack of swiftly flowing water as compared to much of the rest of the New. But this section also features some good bank cover in the form of wood and numerous elodea and water willow beds concentrate smallies in the warm weather period. This getaway is in a decidedly urban setting for the most part, so the scenery is somewhat limited in many places. All in all, the Claytor Lake Dam float is a good trip. After the Class I-II rapid, you will pass another island. There are some water willow beds and then you'll pass under a power line. The next mile or so of this float is very uninspiring in terms of scenery but the fishing can be good although not much current exists. In places, shallow mud flats exist

A great deal of the Claytor Lake Dam float takes place fairly near civilization.

and the water flows very slowly. An industry-owned ramp can be spotted on river right, while on the left several hundred yards downstream, junk cars are part of the scenery. Another power line crosses the stream in the vicinity of the automobiles. Massive grass beds often form in this part of the river during the summer but the New flows so slowly that smallmouth fishing is poor even among the vegetation. The only saving grace for this section of the river is a few scattered water willow beds. I recommend that both canoeists and float fishermen paddle quickly through this stretch.

The fishing potential is good above the Route 11 Bridge, which indicates you are coming to the end of the Claytor Lake Dam trip. First a ledge crosses the river and offers the first real "bassy" cover in a long time. Some scattered laydowns speckle the river-left bank, and a train trestle crosses the river, as well. Near the trestle are some old bridge abutments; cast to the current breaks behind all these structures. The Route 11 Bridge then crosses the New and the riffles above and below the trestle potentially hold smallies. The Bissett Park access point lies within this area on river right.

14 Bissett Park to Peppers Ferry Bridge

TRIP: Bissett Park to Peppers Ferry Bridge

DISTANCE: Six miles

MAP: Page 110

COUNTIES: Pulaski and Montgomery

USGS QUADS: Radford South and Radford North

RAPIDS: A Class II and I, a number of riffles

ACCESS: The park is located right after where Route 232 passes the Route 11 Bridge in Radford. Once inside the park, follow New River Drive to the access point. The river left take-out is at Peppers Ferry Bridge (Route 114) via Route 11.

Guide Britt Stoudemire says that golfing and solid smallmouth action don't often go together but on this excursion they do.

"The Bissett Park float starts in a major pool and then is characterized by shallow riffles and ledges and one big pool near a golf course," he said. "This float has more shoreline cover than the preceding one does. There is an aggressive rapid right above the take-out that should be run with caution. Note: beware of the flying golf balls coming from errant golfers. The river is strewn with golf balls and broken clubs along this section."

The first really good fishing spot occurs approximately a mile downstream when a riffle forms, and there is excellent "push" water upstream. Former New River guide and good friend Barry Loupe of Saltville is a big fan of push water. He defines push water as being the area where the current increases in velocity just before a riffle or rapid. This is an excellent locale for long rodders or spin fishermen to toss topwater offerings or rapidly retrieve streamers, crankbaits, and spinnerbaits.

Another mile or so must pass before you come to another really good fishing area. Some small bluffs appear on the river-left bank and offer a photo opportunity. At the top of the ridge, you also may be able to glimpse a small "waterfall"; a pipe coming out of the hillside causes this phenomenon. There are scattered rocks in three to seven feet of water through here, and they can all hold bronzebacks. It was in this area that I once experienced a boating accident.

Some people mistakenly believe that river mishaps can only occur in swiftly flowing sections, but in reality humans can commit blunders at any place at any time on a waterway. Three of us were fishing from a johnboat, and a heavy rain was falling that July day. One member of my party snagged his bait and, leaning over the side of the boat to retrieve the lure, fell into the water. This set off a bizarre chain reaction, because somehow the seat I was sitting in chose that moment to become dislodged from its moorings and I too tumbled into the river. When the two of us were once again safely ensconced in the craft, the rain began falling even more heavily. By the time we arrived at the Peppers Ferry take-out, I was intensely shivering. On my way home, even though the rain had stopped and the temperature was in the 70s, I kept my car heater on high. My point is that hypothermia is always a danger on rivers or lakes, even in the summer. Always bring along a dry bag with a spare set of clothes.

The aforementioned golf course can be seen on river left from mile three to four of this float and after you pass under a powerline and pass by where Plum Creek enters on river right in a river-right curve.

An old railroad bridge, a culvert on river right, a Class I/riffle, and some excellent rock cover on the river-right bank characterize the next leg of your journey. This area and that around the aforementioned bluffs probably offer the best fishing potential for this entire trip. At the end of the Bissett Park float, you will come to another Class II that possesses a large eddy on river left. This rapid should also be run down the center. Then come about three hundred yards of flat water and the Peppers Ferry Bridge.

The New River is known for its trophy smallmouths.

15 Peppers Ferry Bridge to Whitethorne

TRIP: Peppers Ferry Bridge to Whitethorne

DISTANCE: Eight and a half miles

MAP: Page 110

COUNTIES: Pulaski and Montgomery

USGS QUAD: Radford North

RAPIDS: Class II-III Arsenal Rapids, an easy Class I-II, and numerous riffles

ACCESS: The river-left put-in is at Peppers Ferry Bridge (Route 114) via Route 11. Parking is limited under the bridge. The river-right take-out is a concrete ramp, off Route 623, via Route 625 (McCoy Road) and Route 412 (Prices Fork Road). Parking spaces are numerous in the gravel lot.

New River Outdoor Company guide Britt Stoudenmire gives an overview of this junket.

"One of the slowest floats on the entire lower New River with the most motorized boat traffic," he said. "It's not uncommon to see 50 trucks with trailers parked at the Whitethorne boat ramp in the summer. There is lots of slow water with excellent mid-river habitat throughout the entire section. One major rapid, Arsenal Falls, marks the most aggressive water on the float. The falls is typically not runnable in motorized boats, and floaters should take extreme care as I have seen unsuspecting boaters crash in these falls numerous times."

Richard Furman of Buchanan says the Pepper Ferry float says the major feature is the "very tense ledge" at the Arsenal Rapid. This rapid, he says, has changed a great deal since he first ran it in the 1990s and continues to change. The best path is to run the rapid on the far right side.

Float fishermen should allow about seven hours for the Peppers Ferry junket, and canoeists should easily be able to negotiate it in less than four hours. The New is still very much an urban river through this section as the stream flows through the city of Radford and by the Radford Army Ammunition Plant (often called the Radford Arsenal). Quality fishing begins almost immediately as a series of riffles and drop-offs appear as soon as you paddle under the Peppers Ferry Bridge. A wooded shoreline exists on river right and a rocky bank adds to the area's appeal, as does a river-left island. Some agricultural land and cattle grazing on river left belie the fact that Radford is close by.

The next major feature is the Pepper Tunnel, which spans the river; this lets you know that you have traveled about a mile and that the Radford Arsenal now owns the land on both sides of the New. Trespassing is forbidden here, and paddlers should not debark from their boats to walk along the shore. A riffle lies in the vicinity of the tunnel and provides some good fishing; anglers should especially work the rocky right bank. Then, you will pass through an easy Class I-II rapid and will have to paddle through a section of very deep, slow water. Don't become complacent, though, because the Class II-III Arsenal Rapid looms, which extends some two hundred yards. My approach to this rapid is to portage along a sandbar on far river right. A boulder juts out from the river-left side, making a run down that side extremely dangerous. Some channels exist in the mid-river section of Arsenal, but so do some precipitous drops. The rapid flows much less ferociously on its right side and over time a sandbar has built up there, as well. Certainly one of the best places to fish on this float is the area below the Arsenal Rapids. I like to fish the swift water about thirty feet below the end of this rapid. Then I toss plastic crayfish, jig and pigs, or crayfish patterns to the current breaks that form. A good approach is to slowly maneuver your boat from river-right to river left and hit as many of those breaks as possible.

The next section of this float definitely has character. A steam pipe "bridge" spans the river, and on river left you will spot signs and a denuded landscape in places. This is where the Radford Arsenal conducts controlled burns. A friend and I were once fishing in this area when a voice came over the arsenal's intercom announcing that a burn was about to take place. We immediately stopped fishing and quickly began to paddle out of the area. Apparently, though, we did not stroke with enough alacrity because a man drove up along the right bank and yelled at us about our lack of speed. When the army tells you to move, do so quickly. Some inviting deep-water ledges and good current exist for several hundred yards below the Arsenal Rapid, so this is an excellent place to angle for smallies. Two final focal points in this area are the arsenal's private bridge and, below it, an outflow pipe on river right that creates a small waterfall.

The next section of the Peppers Ferry float features scattered deep-water ledges, a red light on river left that indicates that controlled burning occasionally takes place, and a riffle. You are now well over halfway through this excursion. The New now forms a river-right bend and offers some periodic drop-offs and fetching underwater rock cover. Railroad tracks are sometimes visible on river right; Route 652 lies beyond those tracks. This bend is also characterized by a picturesque river-right bluff, one of many on the New below Claytor

that demands the attention of photographers. When that bend ends, so does the good-quality fishing for this junket. Soon you will begin to see some homes on the river-right shore, the water slows noticeably, and two islands come into view, which are followed by a third island downstream. Plenty of paths exist between these islands, but for the most part, their lack of cover equates to poor fishing. Paddle quickly through here until you pass Toms Creek entering on river right, and soon afterwards come to the river-right take-out at Whitethorne.

Arsenal Rapids, shown here, is the high point of the Pepper's Ferry trip.

16 Whitethorne to McCoy Falls (Big Falls)

TRIP: Whitethorne to McCoy Falls

DISTANCE: Seven miles

MAP: Page 110

COUNTIES: Pulaski, Montgomery, and Giles

USGS QUADS: Radford North and Eggleston

RAPIDS: Numerous riffles, Class III-IV McCoy Falls comes after the end of the trip

ACCESS: The river-right put-in is a concrete ramp, off Route 623, via Route 625 (McCoy Road) and Route 412 (Prices Fork Road). Numerous parking spaces exist in the gravel lot. The river-right take-outs are nothing more than pull-offs off Route 625 above and below McCoy Falls.

The Whitethorne junket has interesting contrasts between its first and second halves, and has different personalities during different times of the year. Anglers will want to spend about seven hours on the Whitethorne getaway. Paddlers can easily scoot through this getaway in less than four hours, but they may want to play in the numerous ledges/riffles and allot more time.

Note: *This section is also a traditional playground of Radford College and Virginia Tech students, especially the area above McCoy Falls; pleasure craft and inner tubes are common on summer weekends. Guide Britt Stoudenmire offers his overview.*

"The Whitethorne float is slow on the front side and ledge-filled on the bottom side," he said. "There are lots of float, wading, and motorized boat traffic on this section. Known for the musky, this trip has seen smallmouths take a back seat as muskies have flourished in this slow water. Tubers dot the lower end of the falls. **Note:** a stiff headwind can make this a long and strenuous paddle once you hit the 'Belspring Pool' area which is basically a lake."

I agree with Britt's description, especially about the headwinds. The wind always seems to be blowing upstream here, making paddling tiring especially if you have combined this getaway with another one. Richard Furman, who guides on the James, notes that much of the Whitethorne float is muskie water.

"I would say that the Whitethorne float is the most well-known trip for muskie on the lower New in Virginia," he said. "The slow, deep water at and below the Whitethorne ramp is like a slow moving lake with rocks, trees, and grass—just perfect muskie water. It's so accessible to the ramp that it gets a lot of fishing pressure from fishermen in motorboats."

The first three-mile section of this trip is well-known for its winter fishing for muskies and both largemouth and smallmouth bass. Motor boaters like to access the river at Whitethorne and work that portion of the New. Indeed, the Whitethorne area has traditionally produced outstanding cold weather sport with largemouths topping seven pounds and smallmouths surpassing five pounds. In the spring of 1998, for example, a nearly 7 ½-pound bronzeback was caught from this area. Hardcore muskie anglers sometimes spend an entire winter day near the ramp making dozens of casts to the numerous laydowns that especially line the river-right bank. Striped bass are even occasionally caught from this area. But once the warm weather period begins, the largemouth bass followers typically go elsewhere for their sport and the smallmouths, for the most part, vacate the Whitethorne area

The Whitethorne getaway features slow water at its beginning and numerous riffles at its end.

for the more aerated water downstream. Muskie enthusiasts turn to fishing this locale at night. After you put in, note the twin concrete towers on river left and a cement structure in the middle of the river. Mid-river riffles and rock cover also appear over those first three miles, but for the most part, this portion features very slow moving water.

In fact, the Whitethorne area is so well-known for producing big fish that the reputation of the area alone can cloud your judgment. For example, before a July float, I had regaled my boating companion, Terry Plesonko of Mount Sidney, about the trophy fish that prowl within sight of the Whitethorne ramp. We had just come to the first riffle below the put-in and saw a school of predatory fish herding baitfish against the bank and slaughtering them. The hapless minnows were leaping in fear from the water. I foolishly told Terry that we might be witnessing a school of striped bass in action. We tossed our topwaters into the commotion—and immediately caught a tiny smallmouth and an undersized rock bass. Actually, if you are a smallmouth angler, your best bet is to quickly paddle through these first three miles, making only a few casts to the random riffle areas that speckle this section. The only noteworthy landmarks are a gravel bank on river right several miles below the put-in and the railroad tracks that parallel that same side. Once you spot the community of Parrott on river left, you have just about passed through the slowly flowing water and the first three miles of the Whitethorne trip.

Now prepare for some fun canoeing and some very good fishing, especially during the spring and summer. Over the next three to four miles, you will encounter one ledge after another. During high water conditions, small Class I rapids form at those ledges, but typically by mid- to late summer, these ledges are often exposed in places and you may have to drag your canoe across them. This is an outstanding section for crayfish patterns and jig and pig combos, yet topwater fishing can be rewarding, too. I also must add that the ledges in the Parrott area are where I fished the New River for the first time. I was a teenager and my Grandfather Willie dropped me off at one of the pull-offs on river left that run along Route 600. I spent a pleasant few hours wading this area and catching smallmouths between six and ten inches. Foolishly, I went wading without a lifejacket because in those days, the 1960s, people infrequently wore them. Unfortunately, nowadays, people just as foolishly do not wear these safety devices. There have been days that I have seen over a hundred people wading in the Parrott area, which is also known as Belspring. I recall very few individuals donning a lifejacket. The New River, much more so than any other river in North Carolina, Virginia, and West Virginia has dangerous undertows. Please strongly consider wearing a lifejacket when you are wading or in a boat.

Another interesting feature of the Parrott vicinity is that, like the area immediately below the Whitethorne ramp, some marvelous wintertime action for smallmouth is possible. Well-known and respected former guide Barry Loupe of Saltville likes to launch from those roadside river-left pull-offs and spend hours fishing within forty to fifty yards of the bank and never moves more than seventy-five yards up or downstream. Loupe painstakingly crawls a Butch Neal jig tipped with a Venom plastic trailer up and over those ledges. Loupe has been known to catch several dozen smallmouths between twelve and twenty-two inches over the course of a winter's day.

A more complete description of the last three to four miles of the Whitethorne junket is now in order. When this section begins, you will note some scattered boulders above a riffle as well as some sycamores that line the river-right bank. As earlier mentioned, you will be able to see the community of Parrott on the river-left bank. Next you will come to a series of ledges that crisscross the river; numerous chutes exist and a seemingly infinite number of passageways are also possible. The next major feature is a large island on the left side of the river. This is a stupendous place to stop and take pictures of the river-left mountain that borders the New. This island is also a favorite area of Canada geese, which frequent this area in great numbers. Downstream from this island are several small islets and a river-left bank where the water willow grows in great profusion; meanwhile, the ledges and the drop-offs below them extend all the way across the river. The water is so shallow through here that during the summer some people wade entirely across the river. Because this section receives so much wade fishing and pleasure boating pressure during the summer, I recommend that serious fishermen not come here on weekends. I recommend that canoeists who like solitude avoid the Whitethorne trip then, as well. This is a great excursion during the middle of the week, but on weekends, the masses of people may be too much to contend with.

You will know that you are coming to the end of the Whitethorne float when you spot the New River Junction, a tube rental concern, on river right. It was in this area that a friend and I once observed a school of two-pound smallmouths viciously feeding on some emerging damselflies. The hatch took place over the course of the noon hour, and throughout that period we cast repeatedly to the feeding smallies. I have often seen that noontime surface feeding frenzy on the New and other rivers. On lakes, the noon hour often brings the end of the fishing day, but on rivers in the summer, twelve o'clock often signals the beginning of a series of hatches. As you near the end of the Whitethorne float, begin making your way to the river-right shoreline. Besides being able to see New River Junction, you will also be able to hear the roar of McCoy Falls as it echoes across the mountains that envelope both sides of the river there. McCoy Falls, also known as Big Falls, is a possible Class IV on its river-left side, and the current along that bank is very strong, thus the need to be on the opposite side as you approach the falls. I once ran McCoy Falls on river left and will not do so again. I had told my boat mate about the intensity of the rapid, particularly on its left side, but he had confidently announced that his craft could run it. We turned over a few seconds after entering the rapid, one of my rods and tackle boxes disappearing forever. By the time I was able to reach (and cling to) a rock, I was some fifty yards downstream, scared and badly bruised. I strongly recommend that you portage McCoy Falls on river right. That side also offers the best chutes. The Whitethorne excursion definitely contrasts from summer to winter, from its first half to its second, and from weekdays to weekends.

17 McCoy Falls (Big Falls) to Eggleston

TRIP: McCoy Falls to Eggleston

DISTANCE: Two and a half miles

MAP: Page 110

COUNTIES: Montgomery and Giles

USGS QUADS: Radford North and Eggleston

RAPIDS: Two Class II, several Class I, and numerous riffles

ACCESS: The river-right put-ins are nothing more than pull-offs off Route 625 (McCoy Road) above and below McCoy Falls. The river-left take-outs off Route 622 are also roadside pull-offs upstream from the Route 730 Bridge. Parking is very limited at both access points.

The McCoy Falls trip makes for an excellent after-work getaway of a few hours for the angler. Although paddlers will find this a delightful trip, it is so short in length that I recommend combining this junket with the Eggleston to Pembroke run for a fun morning or afternoon sojourn on the New. Guide Britt Stoudenmire of the New River Outdoor Company agrees and describes this excursion as a great half day float and that the ledges within harbor lots of smallmouths. He also says that the float receives quite a bit of traffic. Indeed on one float, I caught a nearly 22-inch smallmouth from one of those ledges. The fish fell for a Case Plastics Magic Stik. One other aspect of note is that this float is known for its wildlife.

"I once saw a bear swim across the river and climb onto the island below the falls where campers were camping," said Britt. "There was no doubt he had a routine of checking the campsites for food."

James River guide Richard Furman says that he likes the float because it is so short in length that he can spend a lot of time in the best locales. Richard adds that if he has a full day at his disposal, he combines this one with the Eggleston to Pembroke junket.

Actually, the fishing can be so good on this trip that the unhurried angler could choose to spend a full afternoon here. As an aside, I believe that whether you are a fly or a spin fisherman, you are likely to catch more quality fish if you are a pattern fisherman who moves quickly from one spot to another. For example, let's suppose that you have determined that the smallmouths are feeding on crayfish and that the best way to catch those bass is on a weighed crawfish pattern or a jig and plastic trailer. Furthermore, you have learned that the smallies are holding behind ledges, in eddies, or at the deep ends of water willow beds. Then I believe that the best way to catch these fish is to work that type of habitat quickly, making no more than one or two casts to an individual spot. An angler should next move on to other similar locales, skipping all types of cover in between.

During my many years on the water, I have seen too many anglers waste precious fishing time, working every little piece of cover, regardless of whether or not it had fish-holding potential. Just as bad and just as wasteful of time is when an angler does catch a nice fish from a certain lie, but then proceeds to make a dozen or more casts to that same spot. The result is usually no additional fish being caught, or at best, a few small ones. Another result from this type of strategy is the angler being unable to fish productive water at the end of his trip because he has wasted so much time earlier in the day. Be efficient with your time; make the first cast to an area your best one. After a cast or two to that spot, move on. Now please note that I am not saying that it never pays to "sit on a hole." But for most anglers, most of the time, the best approach is to move quickly from location to location. That is the best formula, percentage wise, for catching bigger bronzebacks.

The fishing below Big Falls can be phenomenal.

After you put in below McCoy Falls, be sure to linger in the eddies and pools that form below this drop in the stream bottom. I have had some outstanding mornings fishing below this rapid. Some grass beds exist below McCoy, especially on river left, and they serve as great morning hangouts for smallmouths. Also of note is the presence of arrowweed along that shoreline, one of the few places that this aquatic plant grows on the New. Not far below the falls is a marvelous mid-river riffle and pool, and this too is a likely smallmouth hot spot. There is an island on the left side of the river. The river-left side of the island is fairly shallow; the best passage is to the right. The island itself is yet another good place to work a fly or lure, especially during low light conditions. The current here creates some very well-aerated water.

The next major feature is a Class I-II ledge rapid, which occurs about a mile into the trip. The best path is on far river left. A number of large rocks also punctuate the right side of this rapid. You will then encounter a series of mid-river riffles and pools, all of which harbor bronzebacks. Some water willow and good-sized rocks especially dot the river-left bank, as well. The superb smallmouth habitat continues when you come to a series of small Class I-II ledge rapids. Next, the New forms a river-right bend, and the deep water in this area is a fine place to toss weighted nymphs and plastic worms in the spring. This is the Goodwin's Ferry area and numerous campers and small buildings dominate the river-right shoreline. Route 625 continues to parallel the river on river right and Route 622 does the same on the left side, giving access to the river for wade fishermen.

The last major feature of the McCoy Falls trip occurs next: a Class II ledge with a three-foot drop on its right side. Be sure to run this rapid on far river left. Below this rapid is a small island and a very rocky pool that is yet another super place to use weighed nymphs and soft plastic baits. Yet one more enticing fishing hole exists on this excursion; below some small bluffs there are some fetching deep-water drop-offs and half-submerged boulders. Carolina-rigged lizards and grubs are the tickets here, as well as weighted streamers on a sink tip line. Canoeists and photographers will relish taking note and/or pictures of these bluffs, a preview of the even more awe-inspiring cliffs on the Eggleston getaway. Finally, I must warn you that brisk winds often plague the McCoy float. The towering mountains that envelop the river create a kind of wind tunnel, and the prevailing wind often blows upstream. The McCoy Falls float may be short, but it is long on pleasure.

18 Eggleston to Pembroke

TRIP: Eggleston to Pembroke

DISTANCE: Six miles

MAP: Page 110

COUNTY: Giles

USGS QUADS: Eggleston and Pearisburg

RAPIDS: Three Class II, several Class I and riffles

ACCESS: The river-left put-ins off Route 622 are roadside pull-offs upstream from the Route 730 Bridge. Parking is very limited. The river-right take-out is off Route 623, via Route 460. The ramp is concrete and numerous parking places exist in the gravel lot.

The Eggleston float was the first one I ever experienced on the New River, and the one I have taken the most often. Anglers will want to spend a solid seven hours on the water while I suggest that canoeists take a leisurely float and spend three, four, or more hours. Both contingents will revel in the stunning rock cliffs and wooded shorelines, as this junket is a photographer's dream trip. This section contains several Class II rapids that are usually easy to negotiate; the last of these rapids, however, can be difficult to run during low flow conditions.

"The Eggleston float is one of the prettier ones on the New in my opinion," said Richard Furman of Botetourt County. "It's because of the dolomite cliffs that appear below Eggleston. The start of the float is not very scenic because of development, but then the cliffs come into view and they are something to see.

"There is also some really deep water, the deepest in fact on the New in Virginia. The float does get fished a lot, and a lot of paddlers take this section, too."

Britt Stoudenmire agrees about the beauty that exists on this section.

"This is my favorite section on the Lower New for scenery," he said. The Palisades Cliffs, Ceasar's Arch, and Horseshoe Bend Cliffs provide remarkable photographing opportunities. The last falls on the section, Prices Falls, eats more floaters than any other rapid on the Lower New due to the number of shallow, sharp ledges that become exposed in low water. If you make it through Prices Falls, then paddling the 'Pembroke Pond' can be challenging in high winds because there is little current in this area. The boat ramp at Pembroke is the busiest ramp on the Lower New for float traffic, but is a nice, spacious put-in with lots of parking. Avoid it on busy holiday weekends if you are looking for serenity. Note: this is one of the first early-spring sections I float for trophy smallmouths."

The first order of business is to paddle under the Route 730 Bridge and to glide through the riffles in this area. Also at this time, you will see the first of a number of picturesque bluffs, this one on river right. I have often heard outdoor enthusiasts debate which New River float is the most beautiful. Many say the Thurmond float in the New River Gorge, others advocate the Double Shoals area on the Fries to Byllesby Reservoir float, and some nominate the Ripplemead to Bluff City junket. My choice is this getaway with its majestic cliffs and the hawks that are often glimpsed soaring nearby. The river's bottom then turns to pebble and fishermen will want to quickly paddle through a fairly straight stretch before the New forms a river-left bend with a series of small bluffs at its end. Rocks also litter this shoreline, and the fishing can be productive despite the fact that a campground lies on river right. As a general rule, fishing is quite poor near campgrounds because many sojourners at such establishments tend to keep the fish they catch.

The New then straightens and runs fairly straight for approximately a mile. On many streams, including some sections of the New, straight stretches usually do not offer good quality fishing, but such is not the case here. Smallmouths, flathead catfish, and muskie all thrive throughout this portion of the Eggleston excursion. Not only is the fishing superb, but so is the scenery. Some four-hundred-foot-high dolomite cliffs dominate the river-right shoreline; these bluffs are often called the Palisades. Be sure to work the shaded (and very rocky) pools beneath them. This is a wonderful place to hawk watch as red-tails especially take up residence here. Other bonuses about this straight stretch are that the current clips along at a good pace, riffles appear frequently, deep-water ledges and boulders exist throughout, and water willow beds are present, especially on river left. The deep-water habitat is ideal for tossing weighted nymphs and streamers and Texas-rigged plastic worms and ringworms with sliding bullet sinkers. Anglers will want to spend well over an hour in this section and paddlers who tote cameras can easily spend just as long here, too. Look for the johnboats of flathead fanciers to be anchored beneath the river-right bluffs. A Class II rapid metamorphoses at the end of this section and flaunts a number of large rocks; run this rapid on river left.

After some more riffles and water willow beds, as well as submerged beds of elodea and curlyleaf pondweed, the river creates a river-right outside bend. This area is called "Horse Shoe Bend" on some maps, but I have never known a highland river not to have a bend with that label at least once or twice during its length. In any event, more river-right bluffs tower over the New in this area, and the drop-offs out from the shoreline conceal big smallies. Soon afterwards you will come to a two-hundred-yard-long Class II rapid. This rapid offers a number of passages and is an excellent place to fish. When passing through extended rapids like this one, I think it is better if one member of a canoe duo casts while the other paddles. Then after the two of you make it through this rapid or one similar, let the designated paddler have first crack at the pool below the rapid.

The Eggleston excursion offers a unique combination of scenery and marvelous fishing.

More good fishing is a possibility above, within, and below the several-hundred-yard-long Class II rapid that comes a short distance downstream. I have heard this rapid called Snidow's Falls and Price's Falls. At this point, you will have covered about four miles of the Eggleston float. The upper two-thirds of this rapid present little difficulty, and numerous current breaks exist behind midstream rocks. However, during low flow conditions, the bottom third of this rapid can become quite tricky, and possibly dangerous, to run. The rocks that canoeists so easily passed over in the spring and early summer are now exposed, and passages between them are narrow. I recommend that you portage around the end of this rapid on river right. Especially be aware of the end of this rapid on river right; the current can sweep you against a rock-strewn bank. The New then forms a leisurely river-left outside bend (as opposed to the sharp one at Horse Shoe Bend). Satisfying fishing is also a possibility here as rocks line the river-left shoreline. Deep drop-offs occur along the main channel, and a series of riffles dot the streambed. The Castle Rock area is next, and more photogenic bluffs can be seen on this side of the river. When you see the Castle Rock area, that is a clue that the fishing is quite poor for the duration of the trip, or as Britt refers to it, the 'slow water of Pembroke Pond.' Cabins line the river-right bank and you will commonly see many swimmers and pleasure boaters during the summer. You may even be able to observe kids swinging from inner tubes near the river-right take-out. Despite frequent congestion at the end of the trip, I simply love the Eggleston excursion.

19 Pembroke to Ripplemead

TRIP: Pembroke to Ripplemead

DISTANCE: Two miles

MAP: Page 110

COUNTY: Giles

USGS QUAD: Pearisburg

RAPIDS: A tricky Class II, some Class I/riffles

ACCESS: The river-right put-in is off Route 623, via Route 460. The ramp is concrete and numerous parking places exist. The river-left take-outs are off Route 636, which is off Route 460. These pull-offs are just upstream from the Route 460 Bridge and are nothing more than dirt/mud openings in the shoreline vegetation. Parking is very limited.

Float fishermen will truly enjoy this short getaway. Individuals who like to experience a few hours of fishing after work on a weekday will especially relish the Pembroke trip. Fly fishermen who like to dawdle and fiddle with various patterns will enjoy the many wade fishing opportunities. Canoeists will want to couple this float with the preceding Eggleston junket in order to experience a full afternoon of floating.

This is the second-ever float that I took on the New and it remains one of my favorites as I have taken it many, many times over the decades. Britt and Leigh Stoudenmire of the New River Outdoor Company are just as enthusiastic about it.

"This is a short float marked by a major rapid at its beginning, Pembroke Falls," said Britt. "The falls is a fairly left to right flow wave train that can get big in high waters and swamp canoers and kayakers very easily. Several islands and the confluence of Big Walker Creek mark the latter half of the float. When Leigh and I first moved to Pearisburg, we used to float this section in our old blue canoe after long days of shuttling people to and from the river since it was so close to our house. This was also the section I first floated with both Bruce Ingram and Cap'n Jack West on a blustery and cold March day."

Britt's mention of the late Cap'n Jack brings back memories of a legendary guide on the New River as well as on waterways in Northeast Tennessee. Folks who ever fished with Jack still rave about his talents.

Both the paddling and piscatorial pleasures begin almost immediately after the put-in. At the access point, you can hear the Pembroke Rapid, which looms immediately after you paddle under the Route 623 Bridge. This Class II lies to the left of an island, which cleaves the New. The right passage is very narrow, shallow, and studded with boulders, so the left route must be taken. At its top, this rapid appears to be very simple, but a large rock lies left of center at the rapid's bottom and that boulder seems to draw boats, and their unsuspecting passengers, right to it. I like to position my canoe on the far left or right side of this rapid in order to avoid potential disaster. However, don't paddle so far to the left that you run aground on a shallow gravel bar. **Caution:** In high water, this rapid may have three-foot waves that can swamp a canoe.

The view upstream from the Ripplemead take-out.

After you have negotiated this Class II, be prepared to have some fun no matter what your favorite aspect of floating a river is. Photographers will want to capture some resplendent bluffs that soon appear on river left.

If you are a canoeist, the remainder of this float presents nothing more challenging than riffles that occasionally become easy Class I runs. The Pembroke junket moves you along briskly but not so fast that you feel rushed. Photographers, canoeists, and float fishermen will want to take advantage of the islands that appear near the bluffs. These are superlative places to rest and take pictures; for the best passageway, paddle to the right of these islands. Above the islands, numerous rocks lie along the river-right shoreline. In some places, trees extend their leafy canopies and offer shade for smallmouth bass to lurk under. On one trip with Anthony Hipps of Lexington, North Carolina, I watched Anthony catch a number of fine smallies by drifting his homemade poppers under these trees. Anthony would make a subtle cast with his fly rod, then give the pattern a gentle pop. The smallies could not resist this approach. This shoreline brings back two other distinct memories from past New River excursions. Back in the 1980s, a friend and I floated through here, relying on Sneaky Pete poppers almost exclusively. My buddy's theory that day was that if he cast a Sneaky Pete well back under the trees and looked away and not watched his popper, then he would receive a jolting strike. Or as he put it, "a watched popper never gets popped." My fishing companion caught some three dozen smallmouths with his pet popper that day, most of the time when he was indeed not watching it.

On another Pembroke float in the 1990s, a group of three friends and I also found success on this shoreline—that is, everyone except me. My three friends had been catching smallmouths consistently throughout the day on three-inch twin tail grubs, so much so that they had about exhausted their supply. I had been catching a fair number of smallies but had not done nearly as well as they had. Obviously, the fish wanted twin tail grubs that day and very little else. When we arrived at this shoreline, the smallmouths erupted into a feeding spree, smashing a twin tail grub every time someone would cast this bait. My friends received hookups on nearly every cast, meanwhile hoarding their last few twin tails. I begged, pleaded, and whined to each member of the party in turn, but no one shared the hot bait with me. When finally my cohorts ran out of twin tails, they ceased to catch fish. Of course, I had already stopped catching anything, except grief from my friends over my incompetence at not taking advantage of very active fish. They gleefully paddled to the take-out while I muttered the rest of the way. On a fishing trip, you can find out who your friends really are when the bait of the day is in short supply.

After you pass these islands, you will encounter several riffles that are fairly shallow and feature some drop-offs. Just downstream, you will note Big Walker Creek entering on river left. Only a mile or so of the Pembroke float is left now, but what a mile it is. Not far downstream from the creek's entrance, a series of continuous riffles begin. Water willow beds exist in this section, and the fly and spin fishing can be outstanding. Topwater lures and damsel and dragonfly imitations are especially effective on summer afternoons. I like to beach my Dagger Legend here and wade fish around these islets. A really good lure to drift through these runs out from the islets is a Case Magic Stik, rigged Texas style with a 1/16-ounce bullet sinker. Soon after the riffles end, you will spot the Route 460 Bridge and, just upstream from there, several community take-outs on river left. I heartily recommend the Pembroke getaway.

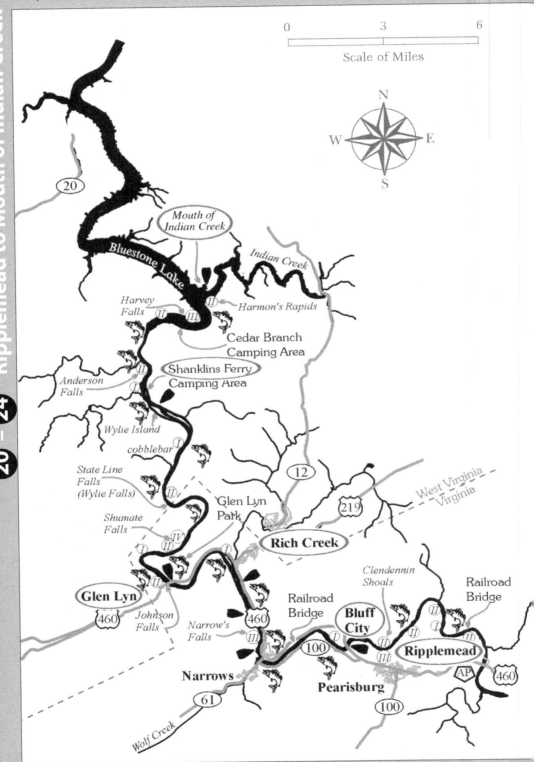

0   3   6

Scale of Miles

Mouth of Indian Creek

Indian Creek

Bluestone Lake

Harvey Falls

Harmon's Rapids

Cedar Branch Camping Area

Shanklins Ferry Camping Area

Anderson Falls

Wylie Island

cobblebar

State Line Falls (Wylie Falls)

12

219

West Virginia Virginia

Glen Lyn Park

Shumate Falls

Rich Creek

Clendennin Shoals

Railroad Bridge

Glen Lyn

460

Johnson Falls

Narrow's Falls

460

Railroad Bridge

Bluff City

Ripplemead

460

Narrows

100

Pearisburg

AP

61

100

Wolf Creek

20 Ripplemead to Bluff City

TRIP: Ripplemead to Bluff City in Giles County

DISTANCE: Seven and a half miles

MAP: Page 134

COUNTY: Giles

USGS QUADS: Pearisburg and Narrows

RAPIDS: One potential Class III, Clendennin Shoals, numerous Class II and I drops

ACCESS: River-left put-ins are off Route 636, which is off Route 460. These pull-offs are just upstream from the Route 460 Bridge and are nothing more than dirt/mud openings in the shoreline vegetation. Parking is very limited. The river-left take-out is just before the Route 460 Bridge. Turn right off Route 460 west, and onto Virginia Avenue, just before crossing the bridge to reach the access point. The take-out is a short dirt incline. Parking is very limited.

The Ripplemead trip flaunts the most whitewater of any float in North Carolina or Virginia, says guide Ken Trail of Rock on Charters, and I agree as does Britt Stoudenmire. I recommend that you either be a kayaker, a rafter, or an expert canoeist to attempt this excursion. The water flows so swiftly that boaters can easily complete this trip in three hours. Float fishermen can complete the Ripplemead getaway in six or seven hours. Wade and bank fishermen like to work the area just upstream from the Route 460 Bridge at the put-in. In fact, bank fishermen often line both sides of the river during the warm weather period and at night when after catfish. Immediately below the bridge, you will spot a power line and the remains of an old concrete bridge support as well as a riffle. Wade fishermen infrequently go beyond this point as the next mile of the New features very deep, slow water. A fair amount of rock cover lies along the river-right bank during this stretch, but far better fishing exists downstream.

"A key to doing well on this float is to fish the pools below the rapids," said Trail. "Most of these rapids end in deep pools with rock cover and a strong current. Fishermen who realize that this is big bass cover are the ones who do best."

Stoudenmire weighs in.

"The Ripplemead float, or more affectionately known as Ripp to Bluff by paddlers, receives the most float traffic on the Lower New River," he said. "Lots of rapids and riffles characterize the section with pretty swift flow the entire

length to carry you through. Clendenin Shoals is the largest rapid on the float
with 'wavey' drops. I've chased canoers down on this section who have missed
the Ripplemead access point or who have taken off with our crashed boats."

The Ripplemead run is also a favorite with paddling instructors. Beth
Wiegandt, a Canoe and Kayak Instructor-Trainer for the American Canoe
Association as well as being an ACA Instructor for Stand Up Paddleboard and
River Safety and Rescue, takes 12-to-17-year olds every year from Peppers Ferry
to Shanklins Ferry. These
five-day excursions, says Beth,
build self-reliance and, of
course, paddling skills in these
young folks.

"Kids don't have to be
good at ball sports to excel at
paddling," she said. "We do all
our training on the river and
carry all of our camping, food,
and rescue gear. Every day on
the section we float, there is a
challenging rapid. But the
Ripplemead float is a favorite
because of Clendenin Shoals
and all of the Class II rapids."

Kim Saunders, who like
Wiegandt is from Botetourt
County, Virginia, says the

*The Ripplemead to Bluff City trek is one of the more isolated
sections of the Virginia New.*

Ripplemead float is a real highpoint of every group's odyssey. The scenery, swift
water, and seemingly non-stop rapids make an impression on the youth, she
says. Wiegandt's class is affiliated with Camp Bethel and the Episcopal Diocese
of Southwestern Virginia. For more information, contact Beth at YourOut-
doorClassroom@gmail.com. On a personal note, my daughter Sarah took this
same course back in the 1990s and came home enthralled about the experience.

The most dominant feature of the second mile is a huge river-right
concrete tower. A water willow bed exists on river left, which is where I like to
debark and photograph the grass bed, the river, the river-right shoreline, tower,

and Klotz Quarry behind the structure. Soon after you spot the tower, you will come to a Class II rapid that sports standing waves several feet high. The push water above the rapid and current breaks below it offer superlative fishing. Long rodders will want to quickly strip Clouser minnows and weighted streamers through this area while spin fishermen will find success with grubs and assorted topwaters. The rocky river-left bank offers particularly good fishing. The New then slows once more and floaters will see yet another marvelous photo opportunity, a stupendous cliff on river right. On one of my trips through here, I floated with Brian Hager and Greg Cook of Class VI River Runners in Lansing, West Virginia. Hager and Cook are veterans of thousands of trips down the Mountain State's majestic New River Gorge. Yet they agreed that the bluffs on this float are the most impressive on the New. Be sure to capture this bluff in pictures, as well. A river-right bend forms under this cliff and offers more angling opportunities.

The next major feature is a railroad bridge that crosses the New; you have now traveled almost two miles from the put-in. Try to work soft plastic crawfish or weighted crawfish patterns in the current breaks that dot the river above the bridge and that form behind the supports. A Class I rapid begins directly behind the bridge and is soon followed by a Class II ledge. The best path is on far river right. After gliding through the Class II, maneuver your craft all the way across the river and check out the river-left rocky bank. The excellent habitat continues for several hundred yards and is ideal for working rapidly retrieved streamers and crankbaits. The river then slows and elodea and star grass grow in great profusion.

The following major feature is a Class II ledge and a river-left cliff that dominate the area and create an absolutely stunning panorama. I can't ever leave this area without taking a dozen or more photographs. The Class II, which can become a Class III in high water, sports a very pronounced drop and passageways are narrow. The best route is probably on the right. The pool and eddies below provide for more super smallmouth sport; be sure to allot plenty of time for both fishing and picture taking. You may want to portage or have a shore lunch on a sandy beach on river right. Soon afterwards, Big Stony Creek enters on river right and you will encounter some gentle riffles. Much of the river-left shoreline is quite rocky. An island then cleaves the river; the best path is to the right of the island.

Next, the New River forms a river-right outside bend ahead of a long rock garden. This is big bass water, but this stretch is also very challenging to negotiate and is potentially dangerous. At the head of the rock garden, a Class II punctuates the New and displays a daunting hydraulic on its right side. Run this rapid on the far left. A Class I immediately follows that should also be run on the far left. Rocky cover abounds through this section and the fishing is simply tremendous. On one float, I caught a number of smallmouths between twelve and nineteen inches and lost another smallie that may have been four pounds. Fast moving baits and patterns are a must here; and if they become snagged, don't expect to be able to paddle upstream and retrieve them. In short succession comes another Class II and a Class I. The former conceals a far river right boulder that is a real boat buster. If you have any doubt about your boating ability, I recommend that you portage on river left through this rock garden.

Mercifully, the New then slows and offers nothing more challenging than the occasional riffle for the next several miles. The scenery continues to be quite fetching and the current breaks behind the riffles and the submerged ledges conceal nice bronzebacks as well as muskies and flathead catfish. Water willow beds also dot the stream in places and provide more quality habitat. A Class II rapid appears at about the six-mile point, but this one is not nearly as intense as the ones upstream. This Class II, however, heralds that you are about to come upon the notorious Clendennin Shoals, a brutal Class II-III, which can be even more difficult to run during high water conditions. In addition to hearing the roar of this rapid far upstream, you will also see an impressive dolomite cliff above the rapid on river left. That's your clue to tie everything down or to prepare to portage on river right. If you have an expert boat handler on board, you can enjoy some excellent fishing during your passage through Clendennin Shoals, which continues for several hundred yards. Again, fast moving flies and baits are the only options.

A large island then splits the New and signals that you are on the last leg of the Ripplemead getaway. You can float down the left side of the island and avoid a Class I-II rapid at the end of the trip. If you venture down the right side of the island, the best passage through the rapid is on far river left where a chute exists. Congratulations, you will have just survived the rowdiest section of the New River in Virginia.

21 Bluff City to Rich Creek

TRIP: Bluff City to Rich Creek

DISTANCE: Five and a half miles

MAP: Page 134

COUNTY: Giles

USGS QUAD: Narrows

RAPIDS: Class III-IV Narrows Falls, a Class I, and riffles

ACCESS: The river-left put-in is just before the Route 460 Bridge. Turn right off Route 460 west, and onto Virginia Avenue, just before crossing the bridge to reach the put-in. Two river-left take-outs exist—both are off Route 649, via Route 61, and offer concrete ramps and numerous parking spaces. The first is less than a mile above Narrows Falls at Camp Success, a public park. The second is several hundred yards below Narrows Falls.

The Bluff City float is a fun paddle of several hours for beginning and intermediate canoeists, as long as they take out above Narrows Falls. Only rafters, kayakers, and expert canoeists should attempt Narrows Falls. Outfitter Britt Stoudenmire says that no major features exist on this float except for Narrows Falls, the most intense drop on the Lower New "that usually eats boats that try to pass through." Fishermen will find this a good morning or afternoon float trip, but not a great one. The first major landmark is the Celanese Plant on river right. In decades past, the plant has been a major source of air pollution. Steps have been taken to alleviate this problem, and only after the passage of time will we know how effective they were.

Immediately after you put-in, you will pass under the Route 460 Bridge and see a beautiful river-left shoreline that is lined with rocks and trees. A small bluff also overlooks this bank. This area often holds bass during the morning and evening hours as several drop-offs exist and aquatic vegetation, especially elodea, grows in great profusion. During the low light period, toss hair bugs and poppers to this bank as well as Rebel Pop'Rs and Pop'N Images. The river-right bank offers very limited habitat, and you will also see several plant buildings on that shoreline.

The next major feature is a Class I rapid that extends for about a hundred yards. The water willow beds on river left above the rapid offer good habitat, as do the submerged rocks in mid-river. This area is a superb place to watch waterfowl as Canada geese, mallards, and wood ducks will often be in the area. An island lies on the right. The rapid itself is what I call a "roller coaster"—one with many waves. The person in the bow should expect to be doused from time to time, but the ride, though bumpy, is not hazardous. Below the rapid, anglers will want to work an eddy that extends along the river-right bank for well over a hundred yards. Bank fishermen access this area from Route 460, which parallels the shoreline for most of the Bluff City getaway. Large rocks line the shoreline and elodea and curly leaf pondweed thrive throughout.

A summer morning on the Bluff City to Rich Creek trip.

Finally, the eddy ends as a riffle begins. This area is one of the better places to fish on the Bluff City trip. Some people like to bring along an anchor to slow their progress through water like this. But I like to paddle out to mid-river and turn my canoe sideways into the current. The added drag sufficiently slows my progress, and I don't have to bother with letting out and retrieving an anchor. Quite frankly, I loathe anchors; besides being cumbersome, they also can be dangerous. Too many times I have seen float fishermen toss anchors out while in heavy current. The anchor often becomes snagged on the bottom and when that occurs, the drag rope sometimes tightens to such a degree that all of the craft's occupants are tossed into the river as the canoe overturns or rocks dangerously from side to side. I won't allow anchors in my Dagger Legend, and I try to discourage others from taking these weights when I am in another person's canoe. On one trip down the New, I tried to talk my friend out of toting along his anchor. He persisted; I relented, and we spent the day hauling the blame thing about. My buddy never saw a place where he thought he could drop the albatross safely. Finally, we arrived at the take-out and began to carry the canoe to a vehicle, both of us having forgotten that the anchor was still in the boat. When we turned the canoe over to begin the process of putting it on top of the vehicle, the anchor fell out and landed squarely on my left foot. Again, I hate anchors.

The next major feature is a railroad bridge; you will have covered over two miles of the Bluff City float. For the next two miles or so until you reach the Route 61 Bridge, you will encounter very slow water that runs anywhere from one to eight feet deep. A large trailer park dominates the river-right shoreline, and scattered fields lie along the opposite bank. This area receives fairly heavy fishing pressure, especially during the summer months, and smallmouth bass action is fair at best. Muskie fishermen, however, often enjoy some success here during the cold water period, and some large flathead catfish have come from this long pool, as well.

Not far below the Route 61 Bridge, Wolf Creek enters on river left. Some water willow beds lie below the creek's entrance and numerous basketball-sized rocks exist in the mid-river region. The excellent cover and current continue until you reach the top of the Class III-IV Narrows Falls. This is a great place to cast streamers and grubs as the water clips along at a good pace. Unfortunately, I recommend that most floaters forego most of this section and take out at the river-left ramp at Camp Success. This ramp lies a hundred yards or so downstream from the entrance of Wolf Creek. Narrows Falls itself offers a difficult portage, and after Camp Success there is simply no good place to take out or portage. Private property dominates the river-left shoreline, and the river-right bank possesses a rather steep, rocky and/or tree-covered shoreline. It is possible, although not recommended, to drag your boat along the far river right side of Narrows Falls, but even there the current is extremely swift and deep drop-offs exist.

The top of Narrows Falls offers Class II water, which is followed by some very swift water and then the falls proper. At the head of the falls proper, a concrete structure on river left hints of the danger to come as the streambed drops precipitously there. (All in all, the streambed drops approximately seven feet over some fifty yards.) The conventional wisdom says to enter the main part of Narrows Falls from the right, then maneuver your way left while looking for openings so that you can navigate down the center. Avoid the left side near the concrete structure. My advice is to take out at the Camp Success ramp. If you do continue through Narrows Falls, or portage on river right, the alternate take-out lies on river left several hundred yards below the Class III-IV rapid.

22 Rich Creek to Glen Lyn

TRIP: Rich Creek to Glen Lyn

DISTANCE: Five miles

MAP: Page 134

COUNTY: Giles

USGS QUADS: Narrows and Peterstown

RAPIDS: Three easy Class I and riffles

ACCESS: Two river-left put-ins exist; both are off Route 649, via Route 61, and offer concrete ramps and abundant parking. The first is less than a mile above Narrows Falls at Camp Success, a public park. The second is several hundred yards below Narrows Falls. There is also a river-right access point just off Route 460 and below Narrows Falls. The ramp is concrete and parking is available. The river-right take-out is a concrete ramp in Glen Lyn Park, located just off Route 460 and just above the Route 460 Bridge. Parking spaces are abundant.

The Rich Creek junket is one of the most underrated and least publicized trips on the entire New River. Britt Stoudenmire of the New River Outdoor Company describes is as "a featureless section dotted with lots of slow water and several islands. Route 460 and two campgrounds are on river right." Float fishermen will require no more than five or six hours to work all the best spots, and canoeists will need no more than three hours. Bank and wade fishermen can also enjoy some fishing as they can access the river from the river-left put-in below Narrows Falls. Perhaps the reason that the Rich Creek float receives so little attention is that it is the last one where a take-out exists in Virginia, and it is far from highly populated areas. The scenery is also only fair as the sounds from scattered campgrounds and houses and Route 460, which runs almost the entire length of this float along the river-right bank, make this anything but a wilderness excursion. Railroad tracks also meander along much of the left shoreline; this is one of the noisiest floats of any river I have ever been on.

My good friend and New River angler Barry Loupe likes to start this float by putting in below Narrows Falls and then maneuvering upstream some three hundred yards to the base of this rapid. Outstanding deep-water rock and ledge cover exists above the ramp, and this section has been known to produce some hefty smallmouth bass. Good rock cover also exists along both shorelines and aquatic vegetation grows in great profusion, especially elodea and curly leaf pondweed. Indeed, during the warm weather period, those two beneficial plants provide superb cover for game fish and their various prey throughout the Rich Creek float. Fly fishermen will find the falls area a great place to cast streamers during the morning when the bass are chasing minnows on top and spin fishermen should score then with buzzbaits.

For the first several miles or so below Narrows Falls, you can still see this Class III-IV rapid as the New flows almost in a straight line. About a mile below the falls, you will note the trip's first riffle and a water willow bed and boulders on river left. Good fishing can be found here, and I like to toss topwater offerings to the base of those rocks. Soon you will come to an island, covered with water willow, on river right. This is a fine place to take pictures or enjoy a shore lunch. Fly fishermen will find this area a marvelous one to work hair bugs, damsel and dragonfly imitations. The water is only several feet deep, and the elodea and curly leaf pondweed provide great shallow water cover. The pondweed mats out on the surface during the summer months, so you may have some difficulty hoisting a nice bass out of this vegetation.

Below the island, you will see a Virginia Game Department concrete ramp on river right. Johnboaters especially like to access the river from here and motor up to Narrows Falls, which is about two miles upstream and still visible. Parking is available in the gravel parking lot. Some fifty yards of riprap exists on river right above the ramp, and it is here that I once guaranteed Barry Loupe that I could

Narrows Falls, shown here, should be portaged.

catch a big smallmouth if he would paddle me close enough for a cast. I ended up tangling with two good-sized bronzebacks, both of which smashed a Pop'N Image. Riprap is rarely found along upland rivers, but whenever this human-created rock cover appears, be sure to work it hard. Some enticing deep-water ledge cover also lies in this area.

About a mile below the ramp, you will come to two major islands; take the river-right path for both of them. After the Narrows Falls area, Barry Loupe rates this section as the best for fishing on the Rich Creek float. However, as is true for this trip as a whole, this section offers little in terms of aesthetics. Trailers line the river-right shore as you float by the first island, and this area receives considerable fishing pressure. Still, I have caught some nice bass here as riffles exist and rocks line both banks. Although I rate the fishing as being quite good along the first island, the angling is outstanding along the second. Three Class I rapids punctuate the right passageway, and all are easy, fun to take, and offer superlative fishing above and below their drops. Chutes are numerous, especially on the left sides of each of them. You will also note Rich Creek entering on river right less than halfway through your voyage past the second island. The creek flows under a bridge as it leaves the community of Rich Creek behind.

For the last one and a half miles of the Rich Creek float, the New flows very lazily along, which is atypical for this waterway. Several landmarks dot this section, the first of which is a large cement block on river left. I frequently see great blue and green herons using this block as a platform to fish from, and wildlife photographers may want to have their cameras ready for the possibility of catching these birds in action. Canada geese, wood ducks, and mallards all flock to this area, as well.

The next feature is a stretch of sycamores and other trees that grow on river right. These trees provide plenty of shade and some fishing opportunities. This area is also good for fishing in the spring as plenty of spawning areas exist along the gravel bottom out from the trees. A third feature is a rather long and very gentle riffle that provides some enticing deep-water habitat below it. I have caught smallmouths in the two-pound range below this riffle and bigger fish lurk. Indeed, the positive effects of this riffle linger for several hundred yards downstream as the water is very well aerated. Finally, you will come to a ledge and a riffle that extend all the way across the river and then four towering cement bridge supports. Shortly downstream is the river-right take-out at Glen Lyn Park. Aesthetically, the Rich Creek float is lacking, but both fishermen and floaters should enjoy this trip nevertheless.

23 Glen Lyn to Shanklins Ferry

TRIP: Glen Lyn, VA, to Shanklins Ferry, WV

DISTANCE: Eleven miles

MAP: Page 134

COUNTIES: Giles County, VA and Mercer, Monroe, and Summers counties, WV

USGS QUADS: Narrows, Peterstown, and Lerona

RAPIDS: Numerous Class II, Class I, and riffles. The Class II-IV Shumate Falls may require portaging.

ACCESS: The river-right access point is a concrete ramp in Glen Lyn Park, located just off Route 460 and just above the Route 460 Bridge. Parking spaces are numerous in the gravel lot. The Shanklins Ferry take-out is at a river-right ramp, just off County Route 23. Parking is available. Note: The shuttle time for this float is well over an hour. There is no easy, direct, or quick way to shuttle.

This trip and the Shanklins Ferry run constitute what some call the "Undiscovered New," that is the seventeen-mile portion of the stream from Glen Lyn, Virginia, to the headwaters of Bluestone Lake. While fishing and rafting enthusiasts come from all over the country to sample the New River Gorge below Bluestone Dam, few know that marvelous fishing and paddling exist above Bluestone Lake. Mark Scott, a fisheries biologist from the Beckley office of the West Virginia Division of Natural Resources, speaks highly of this part of the waterway.

"The section above Bluestone Lake does not receive as much pressure as the stretches of river downstream from Bluestone Dam," says Scott. "It appears that a lot of the pressure that does come on the upper river occurs from people putting small boats on at Shanklins Ferry and Cedar Branch and motoring around from there."

"The upper section above Shanklins Ferry, for the most part, is much milder in terms of rapids than the lower section. However, there are two small falls that should probably be portaged. One is Stateline Falls (also known as Wylie Falls) and the other rapid is just upstream from Shanklins Ferry. I fish the upper New and the bass fishing is good. We catch quite a few fish and usually several over twelve inches. The upper New is definitely worth fishing."

Guide Ken Trail of Rock On Charters raves about this section.

"This is a true big bass float," he said. "I think one of the reasons why is a lack of fishing pressure because the trip begins in Virginia and ends in West Virginia. Fishermen from both states don't come here because they would have to buy an out of state license."

One thing is sure about this float, continued Ken. The mountainous scenery, deep pools, and rapids combine to make this a gorgeous float with trophy smallmouth potential. Ken's biggest smallie on this float was a 21 ½-incher.

Brothers Craig and Chris Ellis from West Virginia believe that the seventeen miles of the upper New makes for a superlative two-day getaway. But for the purposes of this book and for practical ones as well, I have divided this seventeen-mile float into two trips. The eleven miles of the Glen Lyn trek is a long day for float fishermen, and canoeists should allot about six hours, which includes portaging time. To fish throughout the Glen Lyn float, you will have to purchase both a Virginia and West Virginia fishing license as these two states do not have a reciprocal license agreement as North Carolina and Virginia do. Fishing enthusiasts of both Virginias can hope that one day the two states will offer a reciprocal fishing agreement for this part of the New. Approximately half of the Glen Lyn float is in the Old Dominion.

Although the best fishing, in my opinion, occurs after the New courses over Wylie or Stateline Falls, some very intriguing habitat lies south of the West Virginia border and that sport begins at the Glen Lyn put-in. This area is a popular place to bank fish as the New is fairly deep and has a good flow. Some fine midstream cover also exists after you pass under the Route 460 Bridge. This cover is mostly in the form of small pockets behind mid-river boulders. The first major rapid is the Class II Johnson Falls, which occurs less than a mile into the excursion. Some boulders also stud the river, adding to the fishing possibilities. In fact, the entire Johnson Falls area, both upstream and downstream from the rapid, is an excellent place to fish. Plenty of chutes exist.

The next focal point is a river-left outside bend, which begins after you have covered a little over a mile. This bend extends for over a half mile and consists mostly of slow, deep water. Some beautiful rock ledges can be glimpsed on river left, further identifying this part of the Glen Lyn junket. On summertime floats through here, I typically see a number of Canada geese.

At about the two-mile point, the Class II to IV Shumate Falls looms. The force of this rapid varies a great deal, depending on water levels. In spring after a heavy rainfall, Shumate can rock along at a Class IV clip. For much of the spring and summer, though, this is a Class II to III, especially on its river-left side. Obviously, Shumate should be run on that side, as well. Avoid the center if possible, although the current forces boats down the middle. By all means, do not run this rapid on its right side, where it is a Class III to IV even during low water. To be safe, I suggest that you portage Shumate Falls on its river-left side. New River Outdoor Company guide Britt Stoudenmire urges extreme caution for this rapid. Many, many boaters have overturned here and suffered injuries.

I also want to add that both above and below Shumate, the smallmouth fishing can be excellent. I have floated through here on a number of summer-time excursions and have always caught good sized smallies. On one wintertime trip with Stoudenmire, I landed a 30-inch muskie, not a trophy, of course, but a fine fish, nevertheless.

For the next three and a half miles or so, several Class I rapids and riffles punctuate the New. The major focal point of this section is a river-right outside bend that provides some good rock cover and some fairly slow water. Finally, you will enter West Virginia at the Class II Stateline or Wylie Falls. Mercer County, West Virginia, is on the river-left side while Giles County, Virginia, claims the right bank. The Mercer/Giles county line runs up the center of the river for over a mile until you enter West Virginia, in the form of Monroe and Summers counties, for the duration of the trip.

As noted earlier, Mark Scott suggests that boaters may want to portage Stateline Falls. The river-left bank is probably the easiest side to do so. The Ellis brothers and I all love this section of the river. Excellent midstream current breaks exist below Stateline Falls; they are ideal places to retrieve a streamer, weighted nymph, crankbait, grub, or a plastic minnow.

In fact, it was below Stateline Falls where the three of us once enjoyed great fishing. We caught bronzebacks up to sixteen inches in some of the slower pools below the falls. For this section, a solid tactic is to toss six-inch plastic worms, rigged Texas-style with a one-fourth ounce bullet sinker and with a one/ought hook. Popular local colors are pumpkin pepper and black, but as I have said before in this book and elsewhere, I believe that color rarely makes a difference in whether a black bass strikes our offering. It's also good to use sink tip lines to dredge the bottom with crayfish patterns. About a mile below Stateline Falls, you will come to an easy Class I rapid, which has a number of passages. This area offers numerous current breaks and backwaters, typical of the New and other highland rivers. And because boaters can maintain their position with

The Glen Lyn float is rarely negotiated by float fishermen or paddlers.

rafts and other craft above and below Class I runs more easily than they can around more intense rapids, this particular rapid is a great place to allot some serious fishing time.

For the next two miles, the New travels a fairly direct path. Three easy Class I rapids dot the river, and they all offer plenty of passages and super smallmouth fishing. You will then note a Class I cobble bar, and shortly afterwards, a series of picnic tables and campsites on river right. These signify that you have entered the Bluestone Lake Wildlife Management Area. For a very reasonable fee, the Bluestone Lake WMA allows streamside camping on river right. Since those campsites looked so inviting on the aforementioned trip, the Ellis brothers and I decided to debark at the WMA for the evening and pitch our tent. That night, Craig prepared a venison dish along with roasted potatoes, assorted vegetables, and a salad. One of the inviting aspects of spending several days on any river is camping out and the pleasure of enjoying good food, conversation, and the sounds of the night and river. Indeed, nearly every time I have taken the Glen Lyn junket I have camped out on the river somewhere along its length.

The Bluestone Lake WMA dominates the river-right bank for approximately two miles, until the Shanklins Ferry access point on river right. For much of those two miles, an island commands the right side of the river. The best passage, and best fishing, is to the left of that island. Two-thirds of the way down this island, another island appears, this one on the river-left side. Run between these two islands until you come to a midstream islet. Maneuver to the right of this islet and take advantage of some great rocky cover on the river-right side. On some maps, the two large islands and islet are referred to as the Wylie Island area. The campsites on river right are listed as being part of the Shanklins Ferry Camping Area.

Next, you will encounter another small river-right island, which has a Class I rapid immediately above and below it. After running the latter rapid, the Shanklins Ferry take-out looms on river right.

24 Shanklins Ferry to Mouth of Indian Creek

TRIP: Shanklins Ferry to Mouth of Indian Creek

DISTANCE: Six miles

MAP: Page 134

COUNTY: Summers

USGS QUADS: Peterstown, Lerona, and Forest Hill

RAPIDS: Class II, Class I, and riffles, as well as the Class II-III Harvey Falls.

ACCESS: The Shanklins Ferry put-in is at a river-right ramp, just off County Route 23. Parking is available. The Mouth of Indian Creek take-out is a concrete ramp on river right, just off County Route 23. Parking places are numerous.

One of the neat things about the Shanklins Ferry to Mouth of Indian Creek trip is that the Bluestone Lake WMA surrounds the river on both sides. Overnight stays are possible at both the Cedar Branch Camping Area and the Indian Creek Camping Area, both off County Route 23 and both on river right. Bluestone State Park, one of my favorite parks in West Virginia, is also located nearby and offers additional camping and recreational options. Float fishermen can easily negotiate this section in an afternoon while paddlers will find that the Shanklins Ferry float takes no more than three hours.

Superb smallmouth habitat characterizes the Shanklins Ferry getaway. The first mile consists of very easy floating as the river clips along a moderate pace over a very rocky bottom. Early in the morning, this is a great area to hurl buzz-baits, prop baits, and minnow stickbaits, and, if you are a fly fishing enthusiast, poppers and minnow streamers. About a mile into the Shanklins Ferry float, you will observe a cliff on river left. That rock edifice signals some fine fishing as the shoreline is heavily wooded. A number of fallen trees along the bank and beneath the surface add cover, as do some midstream boulders. Next comes the Class II Anderson Falls (passages are numerous), which signifies that you have covered two miles.

Some places "shout" smallmouths, and Anderson Falls certainly does. One float through Anderson with Craig and Chris Ellis comes to mind. Craig and I convinced Chris, who was manning our raft, to maneuver the craft into position so that we could fish the push water above the start of the rapid. When our raft came within casting distance of a deep, shaded eddy just upstream from Anderson Falls, Craig and I simultaneously hurled topwater plugs underneath the sycamore-created canopy. My Storm Chug Bug plopped down a second before Craig's topwater did, which probably explains why I was the lucky one with a hookup.

But it was several seconds later before I knew just how fortunate I had been. For that was when a huge smallmouth broke the foggy, stillness of a West Virginia morning with a prodigious and resounding belly flop. As Chris expertly kept us from floating through the rapid (few individuals would want to undergo the trauma of playing a huge smallmouth while running a rapid), I tried to keep the bronzeback partially under control. After two more jumps and some searing, twisting runs, I finally landed the smallmouth, a fish that was just a shade less than twenty inches. After a few quick photos, I released the smallie back into the New River. Smallmouths of this size are often more than eight or nine years old; please consider releasing trophy-sized fish. If you want some bass to eat, think

The Shanklins Ferry float provides great smallmouth action and fetching mountain scenery.

about taking home the ones that run six to nine inches. Smallies of this size often suffer high winter mortality anyway, and a river's fishery is often not impacted very much if smaller bass are creeled. Everyone suffers, though, when bass in the twelve to twenty-inch size range are unceremoniously dumped into a frying pan.

For the next mile and a half, pools and the occasional riffle characterize the river. One landmark is Whale Rock, a huge midstream boulder that looks appropriately enough like a whale. The Cedar Branch Camping Area lies along the right shoreline. It was in this area that on one excursion my boat mates and I were thrilled to the sight of a bald eagle, which had caught a rough fish of some sort for its breakfast. Next looms the Class II to III Harvey Falls. This is a very rolling, rocky rapid and one that canoeists and johnboaters could experience difficulty with. A long narrow islet splits this rapid with the majority of the current, and rolling rapids, to the left of the islet. To the right of this little spit of land, the New is extremely rocky and fairly shallow. If you possess excellent boating skills, run to the left of the island. Otherwise, I suggest portaging on river right. If you are a photography fan, Harvey Falls is an excellent rapid to capture on film. I like to debark from a craft onto the islet and capture any boaters surfing through this Class II to III.

At the four-mile point of the float, the river forms a river-right bend, and once again the fishing can be stupendous. Work the New from the middle to the right bank. Try bottom baits such as jig and pigs, plastic crayfish, and for long rodders, crayfish patterns and weighted streamers. After the river-right bend, the New becomes very deep and fairly straight for approximately a mile. In the clear water of late spring and early summer, you can spot huge boulders beneath the surface. The warm water period is a good one to probe that cover with weighed nymphs and streamers and ultra-deep running crankbaits and spinnerbaits. This type of habitat will not hold many brown bass, but it will conceal some big ones, especially after the spawn. Scattered water willow beds also characterize this section.

Less than a mile from the take-out, you will encounter the last rapid of the New above Bluestone Lake, the Class II Harmons Rapids. Harmons is a very straightforward type rapid, and passages are numerous. A series of riffles and water willow beds are the main features for the rest of the float. Many boaters like to put in at the Mouth of Indian Creek access point and motor upstream to this area. The river is fairly wide through here, enabling fishermen to spread out. The Mouth of Indian Creek take-out is easily spotted on river right. This is a very popular place to camp and the concrete ramp makes launching a boat easy. Some fishermen who own motorized johnboats also like to launch here and travel downstream into Bluestone Lake. However, for canoeists and rafters, traveling downstream has little to no appeal as the backwaters of Bluestone Lake soon begin to influence the New. At this point, you will have reached the end of the second leg of your journey down the New River; the action resumes below Bluestone Lake Dam at Hinton.

The author with a fine New River smallmouth.

The New River below Bluestone Dam to Fayette Station

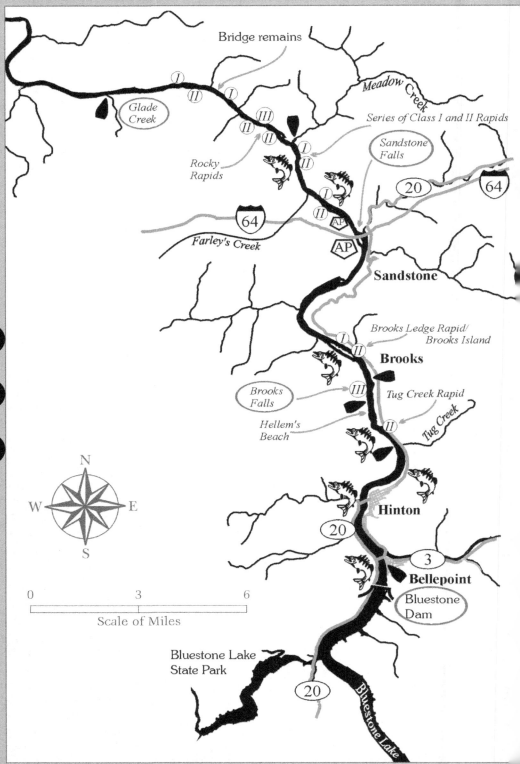

Bridge remains

Meadow Creek

Glade
Creek

Series of Class I and II Rapids

(I)

(II) (I)

(III)

(II) (II)

Sandstone
Falls

Rocky
Rapids

(I)
(II)

20

64

(I)
(II)

64

AP

Farley's Creek

AP

Sandstone

Brooks Ledge Rapid/
Brooks Island

(I)
(II)

Brooks

Brooks
Falls

(III)

Tug Creek Rapid

Hellem's
Beach

(II)

Tug Creek

Hinton

20

Bellepoint

3

Bluestone
Dam

N

W   E

S

0   3   6

Scale of Miles

Bluestone Lake
State Park

20

Bluestone Lake

TRIP: Bluestone Dam to Brooks Falls

DISTANCE: Seven Miles

MAP: Page 156

COUNTIES: Summers and Raleigh

USGS QUADS: Hinton and Talcott

RAPIDS: Class II-III Tug Creek Rapid, some Class Is, and riffles. Class III Brooks Falls occurs below the take-out.

ACCESS: The river-right put-in is several hundred yards below Bluestone Lake Dam at Hinton. The ramp is at a town park known as Bellepoint off Route 3. Parking spaces are numerous. The river-left take-out is a pull-off on County Route 26 (River Road). Parking is limited. Brooks Falls looms immediately downstream.

A little more than a mile below Bluestone Lake Dam at Hinton, the nationally famous New River Gorge National River begins and continues for fifty-three miles until Fayette Station. This national park was established in 1978 to preserve and protect the New and approximately 70,000 acres of surrounding land. This action was a sound investment in the future; many West Virginians realized at the time that the state's future was not in coal mining and timber cutting, but in outdoor recreation. Conversely, Virginia has been slow to protect land along the New River; one result of that lack of foresight is siltation for miles above Fries Dam. Today, state parks, hiking and biking trails, the outdoor theatre at Grandview, and the nearby state parks of Carnifax Battlefield, Hawks Nest, Babcock, Little Beaver, Bluestone, Camp Creek, and Pipestem Resort further add to the area's appeal and create a positive economic impact. Also close by are the Gauley River National Recreational Area and the Bluestone National Scenic River. Indeed, the New River Gorge may well have become the Playground of the East as farsighted individuals envisioned in 1978.

Dave Arnold, one of the founders of Class VI River Runners, which is now known as Adventures on the Gorge, explains the special nature of the gorge.

"One of the most special things about the New River Gorge is its size, that such a large tract of land was able to be protected," he said. "But I think another remarkable aspect is its history. Before the New River Gorge Bridge [an arch bridge 3,030 feet long] connected the two sides of the gorge in October of 1977, local folks called it the 'Big Ditch.' The Big Ditch separated, in fact, two different cultures. The north side was much more rural, and still is today, while the south side, Oak Hill and Fayetteville, was more 'country suburban.'

"A good friend of mine, Audi Critchley, told me that when he was growing up in Ames Heights, he only went to Oak Hill once or twice. The bridge sort of merged the two cultures. Another interesting aspect is the great diversity of plant life in the gorge. Geologists first came to study the gorge in the early to middle 1800s when the railroad was being conceived. Those geologists realized early on that the gorge was unique in its flora. The entrepreneur John Nuttal even wrote a book about this, *Trees Above with Coal Below*."

The Bluestone Dam junket is definitely the mildest one on the West Virginia section of the New.

The gorge boasts the most diverse plant life of any river gorge in the central and southern Appalachians, says the National Park Service. An example of this is the Appalachian Flatrock plant community, which includes species of sedges, cedars, and pines. An excellent example of an increasingly rare bird that breeds in the gorge is the Cerulean warbler.

Although the lower gorge is no place for canoes, the Hinton float is suitable for canoeists. They should apportion about three hours for this junket. Anglers should allot about seven hours. The area immediately below Bluestone Lake

Dam is also very popular with wade fishermen after smallmouth bass, rock bass, and catfish. While staying at Bluestone State Park, I have come there to wade fish and have caught some nice smallies. West Virginia Division of Natural Resources biologist Mark Scott says this area is very productive and boasts excellent numbers of aquatic insects. Water willow beds are common, and in many places the water is only three to four feet deep. However, deeper holes do exist and they have been the undoing of several individuals over the years. As I have stated before, please consider wearing a lifejacket while wading the New River. Every year unsuspecting individuals are claimed by the stream's undertows.

Not far below the put-in, you will float under Route 3 and encounter a series of small islands on the right side of the river; numerous homes and businesses line the river-left bank, which has riprap in places. Every so many years, the river floods those buildings. The riprap and the islands are great places to toss topwater offerings. Also, some excellent bank fishing exists on this left shore; be sure to receive landowner permission before accessing the river. I have stood on this bank and caught keeper-sized smallmouths. The Greenbrier River, a stupendous smallmouth stream, enters on river right amid these islands.

The next focal point is the Route 20 Bridge, which crosses the New in Hinton; you will be well over a mile downstream from the dam. Some fine deep-water fishing exists here; try weighed streamers, crankbaits, and Carolina-rigged lizards to take advantage of the rocky cover. Bank fishermen sometimes like to access the river here, as well. For the next several miles, the New travels along at a pleasant clip as you leave the town of Hinton behind and see fewer homes. Still, this part of the New definitely does not evoke the spirit of wilderness, as the lower gorge does many miles downstream. About four miles into the Hinton getaway, you will spot the Tug Creek access point on river left off Route 26. This is an alternate take-out, especially if you are not at least an intermediate canoeist, because a series of rapids soon looms. Tug Creek enters on river right and the ensuing Tug Creek Rapid, which endures several hundred yards, then greets you. In the summer, when water levels are normal, intermediate canoeists should be able to run this rolling Class II; however, when water levels are high, Tug Creek can become a Class III. Portaging is possible on river left.

A long pool below the Tug Creek Rapid offers some superb smallmouth sport. Generally, anytime a deep, rock-laden pool exists below a rapid on the

West Virginia New, you should experience some fine fishing. The next two miles of the New send forth easy Class I rapids and riffles. The scenery is fairly pleasant as both banks are wooded in many areas, although streamside openings from time to time indicate human presence. This section offers great run-and-gun fishing as you float along. Soon, though, you will hear the roar that emanates from Brooks Falls, a strong Class III. While in a raft, my boat mates and I have run Brooks Falls on its far right side. But canoeists or inexperienced rafters should not attempt this rapid; portage on river left if you plan on continuing to Sandstone Falls. Otherwise, the river-left take-out shortly above Brooks Falls signals the end of the Hinton float.

26 Below Brooks Falls to Sandstone Falls

TRIP: Below Brooks Falls to Sandstone Falls

DISTANCE: Four miles

MAP: Page 156

COUNTIES: Summers and Raleigh

USGS QUADS: Hinton and Meadow Creek

RAPIDS: Class II Brooks Ledge, some Class I, and riffles

ACCESS: Below Brooks Falls, the river-right put-in is at a sand/gravel ramp at the National Park Service's Camp Brookside, located off Route 20. Parking is available. A community put-in is located across the river at Hellem's Beach off County Route 26 (River Road). Parking is limited. The river-left take-out is at roadside pull-offs adjacent to County Route 26 above Sandstone Falls. Parking is very limited.

The Brooks Falls float is the mildest one on the New River in West Virginia and is ideal for canoeists that do not care for major rapids. Only one Class II rapid exists, Brooks Ledge, and it can be easily portaged. Floaters can complete this trip in two hours while anglers will need no more than four hours. Soon after you launch, you will come to Brooks Island, a landmass that extends for over a half mile. Although both sides of the island offer navigable water, most canoeists and anglers choose the right side because it presents deeper water. Bill Handy, who operates Appalachian BackCountry expeditions, says he is always amazed at how the island is such a magnet for wildlife. Deer, Canada geese, mallards, great blue herons, and many other species are likely to be spotted there. The gentle riffles at the top of the rapid are especially appealing to waterfowl. The scenery though is only fair as you float by Brooks Island, as homes and trailers, which are part of the community of Brooks, line the river-right shoreline. Route 20 also parallels the river.

Although the scenery is uninspiring, the Brooks Island section of this float features outstanding fishing. On one autumn trip, which I took with Handy, I caught some nice smallmouths by dragging a four-inch tube across the rocky bottom. A number of riffles and easy Class I runs speckle the river, but the Class II Brooks Ledge is the only rapid of note. Some locals have dubbed this rapid Brooks Falls II as a sharp drop does occur on the river-left side of the rapid. However, floaters can avoid this rapid by portaging along Brooks Island or on the river-right bank. About a hundred yards below Brooks Ledge, an easy Class I/riffle appears in the form of a ledge. This drop in the stream bottom is simple and fun to run and offers good fishing, as well.

After you leave Brooks Island behind, you will note that Route 20 has meandered away from the river-right shoreline and has been replaced by railroad tracks, which parallel the New for the duration of the excursion. The New also soon forms a gentle river-left outside bend. The best fishing, though, exists on the inside bend as sycamores line the river-right bank and a number of steep drop-offs exist. River Road continues to parallel the New on the left and homes and trailers are seen frequently. Guide Handy rates this section as excellent muskie water, especially in the wintertime. Overall, though, the potential for smallmouths is only fair during any season.

About a half mile above Sandstone Falls, you will come to a gentle Class I rock garden. This area can provide superlative smallmouth action as the above water boulders, and the below surface ledges, create excellent habitat. Next to the Brooks Island area, this is the best place to fish on the float. After you leave

Brooks Ledge, shown here, can be tricky to negotiate.

the rock garden, begin looking for the place along the river-left shoreline where you parked your vehicle. Because soon you will hear the roar of Sandstone Falls, which is *NOT* runnable. White signs warning of the imminent danger can be seen from both banks. From upstream, also note that the horizon seems to drop precipitously ahead. After you debark from the river, be sure to drive down to the falls and take some pictures. This is a very striking scenic waterfall; photo possibilities also exist from Route 20 as it winds along the mountain above the falls.

27 Below Sandstone Falls to Glade Creek

TRIP: Below Sandstone Falls to Glade Creek

DISTANCE: Ten miles

MAP: Page 156

COUNTIES: Raleigh, Summers, and Fayette

USGS QUAD: Meadow Creek

RAPIDS: Class III Rocky Rapid, numerous Class III, II, I, and riffles.

ACCESS: The river-left put-in is at many of the roadside pull-offs adjacent to County Route 26 (River Road) below Sandstone Falls. Parking is very limited. Sandstone Falls, located near the community of Sandstone, is not runnable, and must be portaged on river left. The Glade Creek take-out, a gravel/sand ramp, is immediately below the creek of the same name where it enters on river left. Parking spaces are available. This ramp may be reached via the very long, narrow Glade Creek Access Road, which is off County Route 41.

Certainly, one of the most fetching trips on the New River is the ten miles from below Sandstone Falls to the Glade Creek take-out where the stream of the same name enters the river. Float fishermen should allot ten to twelve hours for this float as they will want to linger in the best areas and as this is an exceptionally long trip. Paddlers should allot five hours or so, which includes portaging time. The farther the stream courses through the fifty-three miles of the New River Gorge National River the more intense and more frequent the rapids appear. Below Sandstone Falls (and Sandstone Falls itself is not runnable by anyone) the New is the domain of rafters, kayakers, and expert canoeists. That is, of course, if they are planning to paddle straight through. Johnboaters and other canoeists can put in on private land, if they have permission, or at various access points and travel short distances upstream and down before returning to the access point. I cannot emphasize this enough; the New in its gorge is a rough, roiling river and is not a stream to take lightly. For your initial voyage, I recommend that you contact the professional outfitters and guides listed in the appendix.

Of course, the New already receives much national attention, but even more was directed toward the river on July 23, 2000. That's when the West Virginia Division of Natural Resources (DNR) decreed that effective January 1, 2001, the fifteen miles from below Sandstone Falls to Quinnimont would be under a catch-and-release (C&R) regulation for smallmouth bass. First, here is some history on how the catch-and-release proposal came about. According to Mark Scott, a fisheries biologist for the DNR, the process began in 1996 when a DNR commissioner asked the agency to consider C&R for smallmouth bass on the New River. The DNR then undertook a study to look at the smallmouth population, employing fishing outfitters to collect the data. The outfitters kept tabs on such things as the section fished, size and numbers of smallies caught, and hours spent fishing. Starting and ending times were recorded, as well as the put-ins and take-outs and other comments. For comparisons to be made, the New was divided into three sections: Sandstone to Prince, Prince to Thurmond, and Thurmond to Fayette Station. At the end of two years of data collection, Scott then compiled the data and compared the three sections.

"The Thurmond to Fayette Station section had the highest catch per hour for all smallmouth and also for smallmouth over twelve inches long," said Scott. "This section was followed closely by the Prince to Thurmond section. The Sandstone to Prince section had the lowest catch rate per hour for all smallmouth caught and for bass longer than twelve inches.

"In fact, the Sandstone to Prince section had catch rates that were almost half that of the Thurmond to Fayette Station section. With this data in mind, we proposed a fifteen-mile C&R section from the Interstate 64 Bridge to the mouth of Piney Creek at Prince. At the sectional meetings in March of 1998, the sportsmen in the state voted 88 percent in favor for the proposal."

At a local meeting however, Scott continued, a crowd of fewer than thirty people showed, and some two-thirds of them voted against the proposal. The DNR took the proposal to the commissioners in 1998 and because of the local opposition, the commissioners tabled the issue.

In the ensuing year, a new commissioner was appointed, and he pushed to have the proposal brought up in 2000. Because of several camps in the Prince section, the DNR decided to shorten the section upstream to the National Park Service Grandview Sandbar access site (this is the Quinnimont area).

Scott says that the C&R proposal was then placed before the public and again 88 percent of the state's sportsmen voted for the proposal. The DNR held a public meeting in Beckley and thirty-eight voted for the proposal and one voted against. Several people also called in against the proposal, but Scott adds that the DNR has received overwhelming support.

Dave Arnold of Adventures on the Gorge has floated the New some two thousand times, he estimates. He rates this excursion as one of his favorites.

"On this float, the potential always exists to catch a big smallmouth, in part I think, because of the catch-and-release regulation. Another great thing about this float is the muskie fishery which has really come on in recent years."

The first mile of this trek is known for its wintertime sport as fishermen in motorized johnboats like to tool up and down this section. Occasional mid-river boils, a rock-laden river-right shoreline, and a few riffles characterize this portion. You will also pass by Sandstone on river right and see stores, trailers, and homes. An island lies on this section as well; take the right route as the left passage is very shallow.

The next mile is where the quality fishing (during the warm water period) really begins. Above the Interstate 64 Bridge at Exit 139, you will encounter a Class II and then a Class I rapid. Chris Ellis says this is one of his favorite sections

Chris Ellis admires a fine smallmouth caught below Sandstone Falls.

of the Sandstone float; he often picks up smallmouth bass above and below these rapids. As is always true on the New, some of the best fishing can occur in the push water right above a rapid, and the eddies and current breaks that form below a rapid. The river-left bank is quite rocky in this area, and it too can hold brown bass. About three hundred yards below the I-64 Bridge, you will espy a mid-river island as well as a Class I rapid, riffles, and pools. This is great buzzbait water and fly fishermen will want to cast streamers or nymphs in this section— any pattern that can be retrieved rapidly. Also note Farleys Creek entering on river left below the island.

For the next three and a half miles until you come to where Meadow Creek enters on river right, the New is remarkably similar in terms of its makeup. You will have to negotiate a half dozen or so Class I to II rapids. These are all, for the most part, what I call "cookie cutter" rapids. They are very similar in makeup with plenty of chutes, and they all offer quality bassing above and below their drops in the stream bottom. Also, all of them could cause a canoe to capsize, especially in the spring when water levels can be high. Indeed, several of these Class II rapids become Class III runs during high water conditions. This section also contains a number of islets and these are great places to fish, take pictures, or have a shore lunch.

Throughout most of this section, the river-left bank is heavily wooded, and County Route 7 follows the river-right shoreline. You will also glimpse occasional signs of civilization, such as trailers, along the right shore. Bank fishermen like to access the river from this shoreline (railroad tracks also parallel the river here), as do wade fishermen. I should note that steep drop-offs exist in places along the right shoreline. I never wade fish the New unless I have on a lifejacket, and only then if I can see the bottom. The New River throughout its course in Virginia and West Virginia is known for its dangerous undertows. Be careful.

Some sportsmen like to shorten the ten-mile-long Sandstone Falls to Glade Creek excursion by taking out on river right where Meadow Creek enters the New. Doing so reduces the trip by five miles. An access point lies off County Route 7, just above where Meadow Creek enters. The ramp is gravel, and parking spaces are available. During the summer, this access point is very popular with bank-bound fishermen and those who like to use motorized boats to run up and down the river between major rapids.

The good fishing continues below the confluence of Meadow Creek with the New. Over the course of the next three miles, you will also encounter several rapids. The first rapid occurs not far below where Meadow Creek enters. This Class II is a fine place to work grubs, topwaters, and streamers. Chris Ellis of Fayetteville recommends that paddlers find the most prominent chute for this rapid (several chutes exist and they typically lie mid-river) and take the appropriate passageway. Although normally I like to throw crankbaits and spinnerbaits, especially in the spring, I avoid using these baits very often on the New. The river flows so swiftly in many places that an expensive lure or a "designer fly" snagged on the bottom is lost bait. Going back to retrieve a snagged artificial or fly is usually not an option.

After you pass through the Class II, be sure to navigate your craft over to the river-left shoreline. Some outstanding habitat exists along this bank in the form of overhanging trees and submerged rocks. A Class I rapid then comes into view. Note that the pools below these rapids in this section conceal some marvelous smallmouth cover in the form of small boulders and ledges. Pools that have mud or sand bottoms offer very limited fishing, especially if the current flows very slowly through them. But if pools sport rock or wood cover and considerable current, as these do, then they are angling hot spots.

At the six-mile point of this trip, Rocky Rapid looms. The National Park Service lists this as a Class II rapid and I have heard rafting guides also call it a Class II. But as someone who spends most of his river paddling time in a canoe, I rate Rocky Rapid a strong Class III and Chris Ellis agrees. As its name implies, Rocky Rapid is a long rock-studded affair, and boulders jut out of the streambed numerous places. The river-left side offers the best passages, but I recommend that if you have any doubts about your paddling skills that you portage on the left bank. Canoeists and johnboaters definitely should portage. Another reason why Rocky Rapid can cause difficulty is that the river narrows in this section. Whenever a streambed decreases in width, the same amount of water that has been flowing downstream is "squeezed" into a narrow channel. This compression results in the water being forced along at a faster pace and if there is a drop in the streambed, as takes place at Rocky Rapid, then a major rapid is likely to form. This is big bass water and is simply a stupendous place to work your favorite lures and fly patterns. On one float through here with Ellis, he had a four-pounder roll on a topwater offering that he had tossed to an eddy within the swift water. On the Sandstone float, the guide rates the six miles above Rocky Rapid superior to the four miles below it, and I agree. The above section probably receives less fishing pressure, and the habitat is better, as well. Indeed, in the Rocky Rapid area alone, Ellis and I once caught smallmouths up to three pounds during a late spring junket.

The next two miles of the Sandstone float are not typical of this trip as a whole. This portion lacks major rapids and contains only some easy Class I rapids, if that, as well as riffles, and pools. However, some enticing bank cover exists, primarily on river right, in the form of laydowns, brush piles, and some rocks. But if your time is short, this is also the section where you should do more paddling than casting. The next major feature can be seen from a considerable distance upstream: the remains of an old bridge. Those remains are a clue that you have about a mile above the structure and about a mile below it before you reach the take-out. Above the bridge lies a series of Class I and II rapids. This section of the Sandstone float makes for great run-and-gun bassing as you will constantly be able to cast to likely looking current breaks and eddies. If you can maneuver your boat into one of these eddies, then you are very likely to enjoy some marvelous action. In fact, Ellis deftly swung his raft into such an eddy on one outing, and I was rewarded with a three-pound bronzeback that engulfed my crayfish imitation. This brings up another relevant point. Don't use one-sixteenth to one-eighth-ounce bullet sinkers on this section; they will not be able to keep a plastic bait in a smallmouth's strike zone. Similarly unweighted fly patterns are useless. Slide on at least three-eighth-ounce sinkers above plastic baits and be sure to keep them moving or they will lodge in the numerous rocks along the bottom. Sink tip lines and weighted patterns are a given, as well. Obviously, your success will depend on your ability to keep your bait and fly deep in the water column but not so deep that they become ensnared in the rocky substrate. As always on the New, a fine line seems to exist between doing something correctly or incorrectly.

Below the bridge remains, another series of Class I and II rapids punctuate the Sandstone excursion. Like the ones above, these rapids follow along one after another and require that boaters be vigilant. This section always seems to have quite a few float fishermen on it, especially on weekends. Soon you will see Glade Creek entering on river left, and immediately below the stream's entrance is a river-left gravel/sand ramp where you can debark from the New.

The Glade Creek access point is very popular with sunbathers, wade fishermen, and boaters; expect quite a crowd on weekends. Primitive camping is also possible at this access point. Some float fishermen take advantage of these campsites, especially if they are planning to continue down the New to Quinnimont, Prince, or McCreery the next day. The Sandstone Falls to Glade Creek trip is a fine one for smallmouth bass and paddling enthusiasts alike.

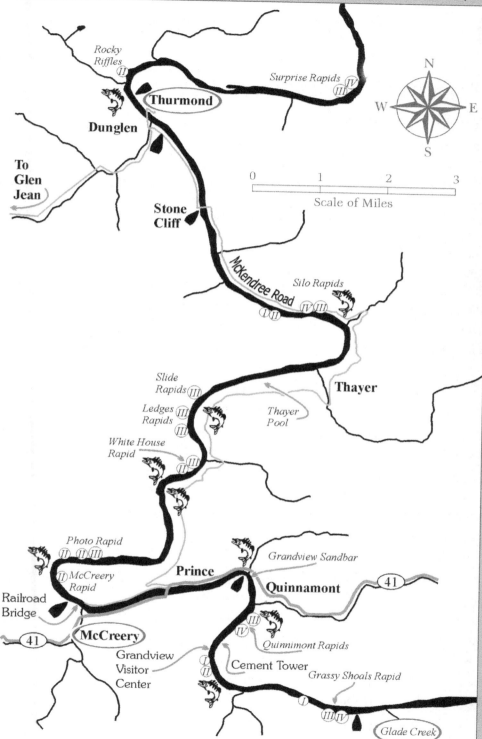

TRIP: Glade Creek to McCreery

DISTANCE: Eight Miles

MAP: Page 172

COUNTIES: Raleigh and Fayette

USGS QUADS: Meadow Creek, Prince, and Thurmond

RAPIDS: Class III-IV Grassy Shoals and Quinnimont, Class II, I, and riffles.

ACCESS: The Glade Creek put-in, a gravel/sand ramp, is immediately below the creek of the same name where it enters on river left. Parking spaces are available. This ramp may be reached via the very long, narrow Glade Creek Access Road, a gravel road which is off County Route 41. The McCreery river-left take-out, which is a gravel/sand ramp, is off County Route 41. The ramp is about ten yards long and fairly steep. Parking spaces are available.

The Glade Creek trek demands a full day's worth of attention from the float fishermen and a brisk afternoon from the rafter and kayaker. Photographers may well find this trip, especially the first five miles of it to the Grandview Sandbar, among the most picturesque on the entire New. Those same five miles constitute the lower reaches of the catch-and-release area for bass.

If you ever have the chance to take this, or any other float, on the West Virginia New during the spring, please do so, says Dave Arnold of Adventures on the Gorge.

"Sometime in late April or early May with the trees having budded out and the leaves formed, the mountainsides turn a chartreuse green that is so intense that it almost hurts my eyes," he said. "I read that the Shawnees had a number of different words for the word *green*, and I certainly can believe the need."

Arnold adds that bird watchers flock to the New this time of year as many species of warblers and vireos have returned for nesting season. Any spring day I spend on the New, I expect to see and/or hear at least 50 species of songbirds. I also have enjoyed spring gobbler hunting in the New River Gorge, though the steep mountainsides are exceptionally challenging.

Before embarking, floaters should know that the Glade Creek float features some strong rapids. The two most intense are Grassy Shoals (sometimes known as Winding Shoals) and Quinnimont Rapids. The National Park Service rates both as Class III, but in the high water of spring they can easily become Class

IVs. "Both of these areas are in somewhat of a curve in the river and, as such, the majority of the water flows on the outside of the curve," says biologist Mark Scott. "The outside is the area to avoid. If you must traverse these rapids, stay to the inside or walk the boat through."

For the first mile of the Glade Creek float, the New River flows very gently and forms a long pool. I prefer to take this whole trip in a raft, but canoe fishermen often paddle up and down this section. The typical plan is to work the very rocky, river-right bank while floating downstream and then paddle upstream and fish the river-left shoreline. The Glade Creek Access Road runs the entire length of this float and provides excellent access for bank fishermen. Indeed, the times I have taken this float, I have always seen anglers casting from openings along the river-left bank. Railroad tracks parallel the river-right bank throughout.

Another characteristic of the Glade Creek float, one that becomes apparent at its beginning, is that this is one of the most scenic getaways on the entire New River. Mountains enclose the stream on both sides, and fog always seems to blanket the river throughout much of the morning on summer floats. The views are often gorgeous and sometimes spectacular. By all means, bring along a camera on the Glade Creek junket.

At the end of that first mile, the Class III-IV Grassy Shoals punctuates the streambed. Boulders exist on river right at the top of the rapid, and the streambed narrows considerably. The river takes a hard swing to the left, which is the most intense side of Grassy Shoals as numerous rocks lie just above and under the surface. In the middle of the rapid, some five-feet-tall waves form and "holes" exist below them. These holes can easily swamp a canoe or johnboat or cause difficulty for an inattentive rafter. Unfortunately, the current forces a craft to the treacherous river-left side or toward those holes. Take the right path down Grassy Shoals or even better portage on that side. Once you make your way through Grassy Shoals, be prepared for some serious fishing. Chris Ellis' brother, Craig Ellis, whom I have taken this float with several times, likes to toss plastic worms and tube baits to the rocks that litter the river-right bank.

The first rapid below Grassy Shoals is merely a Class I that contains a number of midstream boulders. Water willow beds lie downstream from those rocks; and waterfowl such as Canada geese, wood ducks, and mallards frequent this area. That Class I rapid kicks off a series of Class I and II that appear with great regularity for the next three and a half miles until you reach the Class III-IV Quinnimont Rapid. Quite frankly, this section contains some of the best smallmouth bass habitat I have ever encountered on the New or on any other river. And the catch-and-release regulation allows some smallmouths to potentially reach very hefty proportions. Shoreline boulders and submerged rocks, mid-river drop-offs and basketball-sized rocks, water willow and elodea beds, and eddies and current breaks all occur throughout. An angler simply cannot fish all of the cover that exists, but trying to do so is not a bad way to spend a morning or afternoon.

Craig and Chris Ellis look over a smallmouth taken from the Glade Creek float.

After the aforementioned Class I rapid, you will come to another Class I that is best run down its middle where a wide chute exists. Be sure to check out a series of rocks on river right. This cover is a superlative place to toss crayfish imitating lures and fly patterns. Then you will slide through a Class II rapid that is best navigated on river left. Look for smallies to be actively feeding at the top of this rapid in the push water as well as herding minnows in the pool that forms below. The next major feature is the Mill Creek access point. Some people like to take out here at the dirt ramp on river left. Float fishermen who want to avoid the Grassy Shoals Rapid often take advantage of the Mill Creek access point as do those who want to just fish the general area upstream and down from here. This area is also a good one to stop and take a break or have a shore lunch. The Glade Creek Access Road, of course, leads to this ramp.

Not far below the Mill Creek access point lies another Class II. Canoeists can thus experience some good fishing by putting in at the access point and working the area between the Class II runs that lie upstream and down from the ramp. The Class II below the ramp offers a number of chutes. Beware the river-left boulders, but also look for current pockets below them. These are superb places to toss offerings that can be retrieved rapidly such as streamers and grubs. After you make your way through the rapid, check out the water willow beds that dot the river-right shoreline.

Next comes a very easy Class I rapid that can be run in any number of places. This rapid signals the start of a very long water willow bed that continues for almost a half mile on river right. This area can be worked two major ways. Maneuver your craft so that you can toss topwaters to the base of the bed as you float by. If the bass are not lying in the shallow water adjacent to the bed, reposition your craft about twenty yards more out from the bed. Then employ plastic worms, craw worms, and lizards or weighted nymphs and streamers to check out the four- to five-foot deep drop-offs that exist out from the vegetation. Of course, sometimes nice bass will be both shallow and deep throughout this section. But more often than not, they will be one or the other. For example, on one trip with the Ellis brothers, we started out casting buzzbaits and prop baits to the water willow, but we soon realized that the fish were not in the thin water. Chris Ellis then moved his raft out more toward the middle while Craig and I switched to soft plastic baits, Texas-rigged with sliding bullet sinkers. We immediately experienced hookups.

Next comes yet another Class II rapid which causes a 75-yard-long pool to form below it, which in turn is followed by a Class II-III rapid. I have caught keeper-sized smallmouths above the Class II and below the Class II-III, and good-sized fish fin the short pool between them, as well. Run the Class II on river left and portage the Class III on its right side. Once you make your way past the Class II-III, you can catch your breath—at least for a few minutes— and work some boulders that litter the river-left shoreline and some water willow beds and boulders that speckle the right bank. Once again, the river then narrows and an easy Class II is the result. A very easily found chute marks the middle of this rapid and sends you down into the pool below. After running this rapid, be sure to cast upstream and work crankbaits, grubs, and streamers with the current as you drift downstream.

Soon you come to a long pool where the railroad tracks are very visible on river right as is an approximately twenty-foot-tall cement tower below the tracks. You will also spot a small stream or spring dribbling in on river right. Don't let the placid nature of this area cause you to relax too much, as the Class III-IV Quinnimont Rapid soon rears up. Chris Ellis describes Quinnimont as a "heavy" rapid, and it is indeed one that can weigh heavily on your mind as you hear its roar while approaching from upstream. Huge boulders punctuate the river-left side at the rapid's beginning and more large rocks lie at the bottom of the rapid on river right. Several more large rocks dapple the heart of the rapid as it charges downstream. Perhaps the best route is to streak down the middle of Quinnimont, but you must avoid those mid-river rocks as well as several major standing waves that can capsize a craft. I recommend portaging Quinnimont along the river-left shoreline.

Once you have navigated Quinnimont, be sure to enter the eddy that forms a dogleg on river left. I once caught a nice smallmouth there that fell for a spinnerbait that I had churned through the heart of the eddy. Spinnerbaits with tandem willowleaf blades are outstanding choices for working the many eddies that exist on the Glade Creek trek. Eddy bass are active ones and are more than willing to track down blade baits throughout the warm water period. Long rodders can achieve the same result by rapidly stripping a streamer through eddies. The Quinnimont Rapid continues downstream. Below the dogleg eddy lies a Class II rapid and then a Class I. Between those two rapids is a water pipe draining into the New on river right. A few minutes of paddling will then bring you to the Grandview Sandbar on river left, which marks the end of the lower half of the catch-and-release area. This area is a sandbar, and you may observe people relaxing, picnicking, or fishing. Immediately downstream from the sandbar is the river-left take-out, which is a gravel ramp. Parking spaces are plentiful, and many people enjoy camping in this area, as well. To reach this ramp, take a left off the Glade Creek Access Road. The actual site is 1.7 miles down Glade Creek Access Road after you turn onto it from State Route 41.

Although you can end your trip at the Grandview Sandbar, you may also want to continue downstream for three miles to the McCreery take-out on Route 41. As noted earlier, the New flows so swiftly from Glade Creek to Grandview, that the entire five-mile journey takes no more than five hours. The section from Grandview Sandbar to McCreery contains no rapids and is known for its fine spring smallmouth sport. The best action often takes place below a railroad bridge and the Route 41 Bridge, which lies immediately downstream. The New flows very slowly from Grandview to those twin bridges, and a series of gentle riffles dot the river until just above the McCreery take-out, which in fact can be seen as soon as you paddle under the bridges. Bank fishing is very popular in the stretch below those bridges, and quite a few homes lie along both shorelines. In the early spring, target the shoreline boulders, especially the ones on river right, as well as the emerging water willow beds found throughout. From fishing to photography and from challenging boating to waterfowl watching, the Glade Creek junket has it all.

29 McCreery to Thurmond

TRIP: McCreery to Thurmond

DISTANCE: Fifteen Miles

MAP: Page 171

COUNTY: Fayette

USGS QUAD: Thurmond

RAPIDS: Class III-IV rapids such as Ledges, Slide, and Silo, Class II-III McCreery, White House, and Dowdy Creek, Class II, I, and riffles

ACCESS: The McCreery river-left put-in, which is a gravel/sand ramp, is off County Route 41. The ramp is about ten yards long and fairly steep. Parking spaces are available. At Thurmond, the take-out is on river left at Dunglen. This sand/gravel ramp can be reached via County Route 25 (also known as McKendree Road) by means of Route 19.

At fifteen miles in length, the McCreery trek may seem like an overly long one for the float fisherman. Actually, the river charges so swiftly through this portion of the New River Gorge that this float can easily be traversed over the course of a full day. Pleasure rafters can cover this section in five or six hours with time out for lunch and for photographing the picturesque mountains that envelop the New throughout this getaway. Overall, fifty-three river miles of this Mountain State jewel are a part of the National Park System and are protected for outdoors enthusiasts of this and future generations to use and enjoy. The New, rocking and rolling across the Appalachian Plateau, falls seven hundred and fifty feet from the time it leaves Bluestone Dam to Gauley Bridge where it unites with the waters of the Gauley to form the Kanawha. Much of that drop occurs on the McCreery and Thurmond junkets. Furthermore, from McCreery to Fayette Station but especially from Thurmond to Fayette Station, the New is no place for canoeists or johnboaters. Only those individuals who are experts with a raft or kayak should attempt this portion of the New. The exception is those few whitewater canoeists who have the craft and skills to handle this section.

Indeed, Dave Arnold, one of the founders of Class VI River Runners (now Adventures on the Gorge) in Lansing, and Brian Hager, a veteran guide for for the company, believes that this point cannot be emphasized enough. The last two chapters of this book cover whitewater of such intensity that trained professionals are really the best, and often the only, options for excursions. People have perished in the churning rapids of the lower gorge. Second, Arnold and Hager note that the tips for running the rapids covered in these two chapters only apply for when the New runs at normal levels. If the New is flowing at higher or lower levels, a whole new set of variables arise concerning how to negotiate many of the rapids. And, again, a trained professional from one of the commercial rafting companies listed in the appendix would be the best individual to cope with those variables. Another point that Arnold and Hager wish to make is that professional outfitters many times break up the distance covered in chapter five (fifteen miles) and chapter six (thirteen and a half miles). Alternative private access points exist and these are frequently utilized, as are public and unofficial access points. I also must note that for these two chapters I have totally relied on the advice of professionals concerning how to negotiate rapids. I am a canoeist and not a professional rafter and have no business giving tips on how to charge through the rapids of the lower gorge.

Some local anglers like to come to the McCreery put-in and fish from the shore. I often have seen families and fishing buddies wetting a line there. This site is also a good one for a canoeist or a johnboater with a trolling motor to access the river. Both can make their way upstream for several hundred yards to partake of some fishing. However, readers should be forewarned that the McCreery to Thurmond section as a whole is not meant for johnboats or canoes. A number of Class III-IV and above rapids (depending on water levels) exist on this section, and they can easily swamp a boat.

Dave Arnold says that his favorite way to break down this section of the New is to run from Thurmond to Cunard and Cunard to Fayette Station.

"The Thurmond trip offers a diversity of long, deep pools, plus riffle-pool habitat, and then, of course, all the major rapids," he said. "The Thurmond trip also has Surprise Rapid, which from its top to its bottom offers great fishing and white water rafting."

Cunard to Fayette Station is a junket I have taken many times over the years, and the whitewater and trophy smallmouth thrills that are possible are something to behold.

"The Cunard float is more inaccessible with its rougher rapids, so it does not receive as much fishing pressure," said Arnold. "Visually, this trip is the most spectacular with the high mountain walls, major rapids, and canyon-like atmosphere. I like to catch fish, but the major appeal of this float is the 'wow' factor. The water is deeper, swifter, and more constricted through here and the drops—the rapids—are not to be taken lightly. When water meets rock, water always wins, and the tight channels and steep drops are a testament to that. If you are someone who relishes a chance at big smallmouths or if you are a paddler who lives for the rush, the Cunard float belongs on a list of places you have to go on."

Right after the put-in, you will encounter the Class II McCreery Rapid. Excellent bank cover exists on river right as do a series of small pools. Just downstream from there, you will spot a series of eddy walls on river right and some camps on the left side. This shoreline is yet another place where fishermen like to cast from shore. It is possible for anglers to catch some very nice bronze-backs from the bank there, especially in the spring if the river is not high or muddy. Often, though, the best fishing for three-to-five-pound smallies comes in mid-river, right above and below major rapids. This is true not only in this section, but also throughout the McCreery to Thurmond trek.

Two more major rapids lie near the end of the first mile of this excursion; both Class II to III in strength and both occurring in a river-left bend. For the first one, work the eddies on river left as well as some excellent bank cover on that side. This is a superb place for long rodders to strip streamers quickly just under the surface or spin fishermen to retrieve buzzbaits rapidly across the top. The second of these swift water sections is known as Photo Rapid. This is a popular place for scenic photographers and/or those wishing to capture their New River junket. Eddies dot the river-left side below Photo Rapid, and some enticing fishing exists for quite a few yards below, as well. This is by far the most difficult rapid on the first mile of the McCreery junket.

On the second mile of the float, floaters will note that shoreline development becomes much less frequent and that trend continues for the rest of the trip. Basically, long pools with only a few swift water places characterize this section. This portion is a good one for float fishermen to take matters easy and cast occasionally to shoreline cover such as scattered rocks and overhanging tree branches. The next mile of this getaway hosts only one major rapid, a Class II to III that comes near the end of this section. This is a rolling, roller coaster of a rapid. You will also spot a number of boulders on river left. Mountains envelop the New through there, and river runners begin to experience the splendid isolation of the gorge.

The next major rapid comes about one-third of the way through this float. This is commonly called White House Rapid because nearby on river left is a white domicile. The guide further describes this rapid as "a real boat-keeper" because of the hydraulic that lurks within it. The Class II to III White House Rapid actually consists of two rapids with some riffle water in between. Obviously, anytime a rapid of this magnitude occurs on the New, great fishing is a real possibility. Be sure to check out the riffle area between the upper and lower sections of White House as well as the "slick water" above and below the rapid.

Four points need to be made here. First, be sure to note the railroad tracks that parallel the New on river right. They will wind along with the stream for the rest of this trip. County Route 25, also known as McKendree Road, runs near those tracks. Some individuals use the road and railroad tracks to access the river and fish from the shoreline. Second, if you should suffer a mishap on this or any other river, railroad tracks will eventually lead you to a road or some other form of civilization. Third, the next major landmark is where Dowdy Creek enters on river right. A tunnel marks this area. And, last, the Dowdy Creek area is a marvelous place to fish. Indeed, this area is probably my favorite place to fish on the Prince to Thurmond trip. There are shoals, drop-offs, and some really impressive boulders on river right.

On a number of trips, I have spent quite a bit of time in this pool. This is a super locale to use soft plastic baits such as worms, craw worms, and lizards. Rig them Texas-style with one-fourth-ounce bullet sinkers, and slither these creatures along the bottom. Fly fishermen may want to try weighted nymphs and streamers in the Dowdy Creek area. About a mile after Dowdy Creek unites with the New, you will encounter a series of three major rapids. The first one has no name, but the next two are often called "Ledges" and "Slide." These two rapids are aptly named as some ledges exist within the former and the latter has quite a drop to it. Both are strong Class III rapids and can change into Class IV chutes during the spring or any time when the river runs full. After charging through these rapids, you can now catch your breath for a while. You have reached Thayer Pool, a long, slow stretch some one and a half miles in length that is characterized by riffles, fetching scenery, and some great deep water fishing. A fishing camp located on river right also marks this section. Thayer Pool is a wonderful spot to use deep running crankbaits and weighted Woolly buggers to probe bottom cover such as wood and rocks. Another solid tactic for this section is to employ ½-ounce single blade Colorado spinnerbaits. Allow these lures to helicopter to the bottom and slow roll them across the substrate. Any time this blade bait deflects off rock or wood cover, prepare for a strike.

One of the truisms about much of the New River's gallop through West Virginia is that float fishermen, rafters, and kayakers should never allow themselves to become relaxed and complacent. Just when you think that you have seen the worst of the whitewater, or the best, depending on your point of view,

along comes another considerable rapid. Such is the case after the terminus of Thayer Pool. Buffalo Creek, a trout stream, enters on river right near the end of Thayer Pool and can serve as a reminder that a major rapid is not far downstream. For next on the agenda is the potentially treacherous Silo Rapid, a strong Class III to IV. There is some history behind the naming of this rapid. In the early twentieth century, a silo in this area stored sand. That sand was used to make glass for Ford Model T's, the famous Tin Lizzies of the early automotive age. The British Royal Family owned a factory at this site, and during this time period, the New River Gorge experienced an economic boom. Henry Ford, however, mistakenly

The McCreery to Thurmond trek contains numerous major rapids.

thought Americans would never tire of the functional style of the Model T, which was by no means a luxury car, albeit a practical one. Until 1926, for example, the Model T came in only one color: black. United States consumers, though, became more style-oriented, spelling doom for the Model T.

Today, little is left of the British Royal Family's factory, but Silo Rapid remains, dotting the New like it has for numerous centuries. I like to spend a great deal of time fishing this area. The good fishing actually begins about one hundred yards above Silo; professional guides use their rafts to crisscross the river here enabling their companions to cast repeatedly to likely areas. This is a good section to work minnow plugs and crayfish-colored crankbaits. As always, topwaters such as prop baits, chuggers, and hair bugs should be considered for this type of habitat.

After you successfully negotiate Silo, maneuver your raft over to the river-right shoreline. Fish a series of prime eddies that hold numerous small-mouths. I have caught smallmouths there primarily on three-inch grubs on one-fourth-ounce jigheads. On many rivers, one-fourth-ounce jigheads will constantly hang on the bottom. But in the New River Gorge, I find that I often have to use heavier jigheads in order to enable the bait to descend to a brown bass' strike zone. Don't pass up the eddies below Silo Rapid. Also, be forewarned about this rollicking rapid. Many boaters have experienced serious trouble here. This is no place for someone who is not an expert with a raft.

After Silo Rapid, the next swift water section is only a Class I. On river left is a very rocky, shady bank that often holds smallies. Then you will come to a long, slow pool and will spot a coal tipple on river right. Four rapids comprise the next leg of this junket. All of these rapids are rated Class I to II and they are fairly easy to run, except for the last one. Stupendous rock cover exists through-out this section, and float fishermen should budget their time so that they will not be rushed by the time they float through this section. Over the years, one of the peculiarities of float fishermen that I have noticed is that many of us spend too much time casting at the beginning of the trip and too much time paddling at the end. This is true regardless of the quality of the habitat at the beginning or end of a getaway. My point is that some superior smallmouth sport can be found at the end of this trip. Make sure that you have enough time to probe the eddies, deep-water ledges, and current breaks on this section. For much of this portion, the river-left shoreline especially offers fine cover.

Indeed, on one trip, the shadows had already begun to fall across the river when a friend and I made our way down this shoreline. I was casting a one-fourth-ounce buzzbait to rock cover along the bank when our biggest smallmouth of the trip, a possible four-pounder, blew up on the buzzer. I missed the fish and as is typical, I could not make it come back for a return engagement, although my companion expertly held the raft in place as I made repeated casts. This rock-covered bank, and the numerous mini-eddies and current breaks along it, are good places for you to tie into an oversized smallmouth, too. Some people like to end their float at Stone Cliff, eleven miles below the McCreery access point. Stone Cliff was once a community but is now nothing more than a place name and a large beach; the take-out named for the former hamlet is on river left. County Route 25 leads to this access point. Like the McCreery access point, this one is also a very popular place for local anglers to fish from the shoreline. Rarely, have I put in or taken out here when I did not see at least a few people wading for bass. If you decide to do so at either of these access points, please consider wearing a life jacket. The New has a very strong undertow and numerous drop-offs along its bottom. A slip could result in tragedy. I also strongly believe in wearing my life jacket the entire time I am within a raft or any other river craft. Even though the air temperature can climb into the nineties on a summer trip, I keep the jacket on. The New River is a waterway that must be treated with respect.

After you pass Stone Cliff, you must paddle through over a mile of very uncharacteristic (for the New River Gorge that is) slow water called Thurmond Pool. Still, the mountains that surround the New throughout these two miles are quite scenic, and this section does allow voyagers to drift aimlessly along for a while. Much of Thurmond Pool lies in water three to ten feet deep, although there is one hole with about eighteen-feet of liquid. Riffles characterize this section, and this area is known to produce some big bass during the cold water period. Soon you will come to the Thurmond, also known as Dunglen, take-out. The thrills of the lower gorge now await.

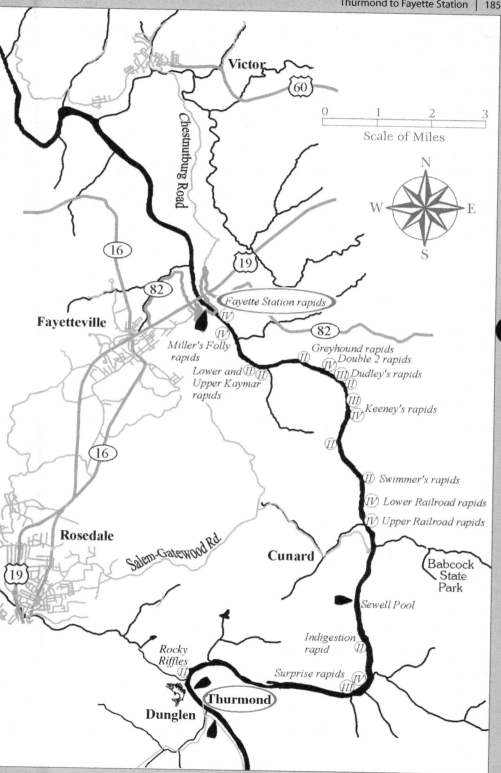

Victor

60

Chestnutburg Road

0   1   2   3
Scale of Miles

N
W   E
S

16

82

Fayette Station rapids
IV

Fayetteville

82

IV
Miller's Folly
rapids

Greyhound rapids
II   Double 2 rapids
IV
III   Dudley's rapids
II

Lower and II   II
Upper Kaymar
rapids

III   Keeney's rapids
IV

II

16

II   Swimmer's rapids

IV   Lower Railroad rapids

IV   Upper Railroad rapids

Rosedale

Salem-Gatewood Rd.

Cunard

Babcock
State
Park

19

Sewell Pool

Indigestion
rapid   II

Rocky
Riffles
II

Surprise rapids   IV
III

Thurmond

Dunglen

TRIP: Thurmond to Fayette Station

DISTANCE: Thirteen and a half miles

MAP: Page 186

COUNTY: Fayette

USGS QUADS: Thurmond and Fayetteville

RAPIDS: Technical Class IV-V Rapids, IIIs, and IIs, as well as Class I and riffles

ACCESS: At Thurmond, the put-in is on river left at Dunglen. This gravel/sand ramp can be reached via County Route 25 (also known as McKendree Road) by means of Route 19. The take-out, a sand/gravel ramp, is on river left just off Route 82 (Fayette Station Road).

Many whitewater enthusiasts from around the country take the Thurmond trek every year. This is the mecca East of the Mississippi River for those who want their rapids high, wide, and roaring. The names of some of these rapids hint of their intensity; after all, when a rapid named Miller's Folly, Surprise, Double Z, or Greyhound Bus Stopper looms ahead, you know you are in for a wild ride. A thriving whitewater rafting business, which includes numerous rafting companies and several fishing guide services, has grown up around the town of Fayetteville, proving that outdoor recreation can sustain an area's economy. Indeed, the whitewater industry has burgeoned into a multi-million-dollar business. Rock climbing, horseback riding, and bird watching aficionados also travel to this area and various businesses cater to their needs, as well.

Indeed, this area is a wonderful place to visit, says lifelong resident Sharon Cruikshank, who is in charge of the New River Gorge Convention and Visitors Bureau.

"I think the New River Gorge is a special place to everyone because of the relaxed atmosphere, it feels like you can breathe here," she said. "All of the unique restaurants are locally owned, so you get a flavor of our community—there is something for everyone."

Only professional rafters should attempt the Thurmond experience. This is no place for a rafter with intermediate skills. The float itself can be covered in four or five hours under normal conditions, but most outfitters take several hours longer to give clients the opportunity to take pictures, swim, and have shore lunches on the boulders found along the shorelines. Fishing trips usually take about eight hours. And anglers should realize before they embark that fishing the lower gorge is a very different experience from any they have likely encountered. Dave Arnold of Adventures on the Gorge, who operates Class VI River Runners in Lansing, agrees.

"When the water flow and the weather conditions are right, the lower gorge can provide some phenomenal fishing," he said. "I have been on trips when the fishing was so good that you expected a strike on every cast. Of course, there are some days when the fishing can be quite difficult here, as it can be anywhere else.

"During the summer, I think a real key to success in the lower gorge is using topwater lures or flies that can be retrieved rapidly. The current flows so fast, that a guide has a lot of difficulty holding the boat in a certain area for long. So a fisherman has to get a smallmouth's attention immediately. That's why buzzbaits and streamers are very effective; they are things that a bass strikes in an almost reflexive manner."

Mark Scott, a fisheries biologist for the West Virginia Division of Natural Resources, agrees that the lower gorge boasts an outstanding smallmouth bass population. Scott says that bass up to six pounds are possible and that there are good numbers of fish in the one-to-two-pound range, as well. Scott also warns "of the extremely dangerous rapids" in the lower gorge. The gorge is best experienced, he maintains, in rafts and dories manned by professional guides. In other words, the lower New River Gorge is definitely not a place where the casual fisherman can put in with his canoe or johnboat and float placidly downstream for the entire trip. The biologist also adds that on weekends especially, float fishermen should not expect to find solitude while traveling down the lower gorge. Given the popularity of the whitewater rafting industry, anglers will have to share the river with hundreds of rafters and kayakers. The fishing is often best, or at least more pleasurable, during the Monday through Friday period, especially during the summer months.

Scott agrees with Arnold about the need to make quick, accurate casts. Anglers will be fortunate to make at most one or two casts to promising areas before the current carries a craft downstream. The biologist suggests that fishermen target rocky banks, points, ledges, and eddies. Eddies especially are prime locales in the lower reaches of the gorge. These tiny backwaters form along the bank or behind boulders and can harbor jumbo brown bass. Even eddies that are just a few feet across can conceal three-pound and larger mossybacks. Often called the "Grand Canyon of the East," the lower gorge bedazzles the eye and stirs the soul with its spectacular beauty and superlative bronzeback sport.

If you have the time, you may decide to linger awhile in Thurmond before you depart. It was a major railroad hub in the early 1900s, and the town was famous, perhaps infamous is a better word, for its saloons and rowdy inhabitants. Two sayings from the past accurately describe the town then: "No Sunday west of Clifton Forge and no God west of Hinton" and "The only difference between Hell and Thurmond is that a river runs through Thurmond." The invention of the diesel locomotive and the decline of the coal industry helped doom the town, and today it is but a shadow of its former self. The historic Thurmond Depot is an interesting spot to learn about the area's past.

For this chapter, I relied heavily on two professional whitewater rafters, Dave Arnold and fishing guide Robin Moore (who has since passed away) of Cast-Away in Lansing; a non-professional rafter like myself cannot detail this excursion as accurately as those individuals who experience it scores of times every year. Just downstream from the put-in, you will spot the Thurmond Bridge, the first major landmark. Pass under the bridge, and you will encounter Rocky's Riffles, a Class II that offers plenty of passages. As the current slows down, a pool forms. The New next forms a river-left bend, straightens, and then come a series of Class I shoals and pools for several miles.

"In the lower gorge, just about every pool below every rapid can offer fantastic fishing," said Moore. "It's true for these Class I shoals and also for downstream."

Dave Arnold agrees, maintaining that it is almost redundant to continuously point out the bass potential in rapid/pool habitat. Both individuals insist that the fishing spots are so numerous that anglers cannot possibly work them all during any given trip. That fact may be why the lower gorge offers such magnificent sport; the bass have so much prime habitat that they can withstand fairly heavy pressure. Just when you thought that perhaps the rambunctious reputation of the river's rapids was undeserved, Surprise Rapid, a 400-yard Class III to IV, looms at the four-and-a-half-mile point as the New makes a river-right curve. Moore counsels rafters who are fishing to stay to the far river left "as hard as you can go" through Surprise. This is not an easy task because the current constantly pushes a craft right of center.

A major wave and vertical drop lies near the end of Surprise, and, in fact, gives the rapid its name. Boaters won't be able to see the drop-off until they are upon it. And by then, of course, there is precious little that they can do. Moore suggests that anglers have all their gear tied down before entering Surprise. Brooklyn Pool forms below Surprise and continues for less than a mile. A series of boulders litter the river-left shoreline at the top half of Brooklyn. Toward the end of the pool, the boulders become much more scattered and a mud bank exists. This side drops off very quickly from the bank. The right side is very rocky and shallow with the main channel lying in water six to ten feet deep.

A Class II rapid appears next. Known variously as Baloney or Indigestion, this rapid offers good fishing at its lip and for a number of yards downstream. Sewell Pool follows and is named for Steven Sewell, the first European to enter this area of West Virginia. Sewell was a trapper who explored the gorge in the mid-1700s. The pool also serves to indicate that you have arrived at Cunard. Cunard is an alternative access point for the Thurmond to Fayette Station stretch and lies about seven and a half miles into the trip and along County Route 9. The Cunard area is popular with bank fishermen who congregate on the river-left shoreline to work Sewell Pool. Rafters can launch their craft by means of two hand railings (and fifty-three concrete steps) that lead to the New on the river-left side. Moore notes that the vertical nature of the path that the hand railings follow makes the launching of a raft "interesting."

"Anyone who is not an accomplished rafter needs to take out at Cunard," warns Moore. "Experienced whitewater rafters only should attempt to float from there to Fayette Station."

After Sewell Pool, the Class III Upper Railroad Rapid begins immediately above a railroad bridge. Moore and Arnold suggest that rafters hug the far river-left side of Upper Railroad in order to avoid the heart of the rapid, which is on the right. A major river-right hole comes at the end of this rapid's first stage, and a series of waves punctuate Upper Railroad toward its end.

After you pass through Upper Railroad and under the bridge, be sure to eddy out on the river-right side. I have tangled with smallmouths up to four pounds in this area, which is characterized by a number of large rocks in water three to six feet deep. Drag a crayfish pattern, jig and pig or Texas-rigged worm through this area. Moore reports that a client once landed a twenty-four-inch smallie below Upper Railroad. Lower Railroad Rapid begins soon after at the eight-mile mark. At very low water levels, says Dave Arnold, Lower Railroad has a history of being dangerous and has caused several deaths. Run this very bumpy Class IV on the far river right; major drop-offs and ledges lie on the left. A pool extends for some three hundred yards below Lower Railroad and is a good place to calm your nerves and make some casts. Swimmer's Rapid is next on the agenda. This Class II has a number of large boulders on its river-right side, and those boulders are popular places to take a break or consume a snack. The New then forms a river-right curve. Four "small," similar Class II rapids dot the river for the next one and one-fourth mile. This quartet (which are called First, Second, Third, and Fourth Warm-Ups) in some measure prepare you for the Class III to IV Upper Keeney which rears up around the ten-mile point. The major feature of Upper Keeney is a gigantic and whale-shaped boulder, appropriately known as Whale Rock, which dominates the rapid's conclusion. Travel the river-right route to avoid Whale Rock. Pinning the boat is a real possibility if you venture too close to this boulder. Middle Keeney churns up next; scout from the right bank. This Class IV is infamous for its huge waves. As Moore said, "Sometimes a guide can keep people dry in Middle Keeney, and sometimes he can't." Lower Keeney follows hard upon and likewise should be scouted from the left bank. Arnold and Moore instruct that you run the middle of this rapid.

"The problem is, though, that this rapid always forces you to the left toward some huge rocks," said Moore. "The further into this rapid you go, the bigger the waves become. I always dread running Lower Keeney; it is easy to break an oar and/or get soaked. Lower Keeney is just one of those rapids that will make a guide look bad. Be careful to avoid the huge rocks at its bottom; some house-sized ones jut out from the left bank."

The Class II to III French Bread Loaf, also known as Dudley's Dip, then ensues; run it center left. The imposing Class IV+ Double Z soon follows at around the ten-and-a-half-mile mark. Start at this rapid's center, go to the far right, then move to the middle, and to the left; in other words, make a Z-route through it. Hopefully, you will avoid the rocks that speckle this section, especially the rock at the bottom left of the rapid. Moore says this rock is known as "Otter Rock," as in "you 'otter' be to the right of it, if you know what is good for you." That rock forms Barry's Hole at high water. Then comes the Class III Turtle Rapid; it can be negotiated in multiple ways says Arnold. The Class II+

Greyhound Bus Stopper must be contended with next. Run to the far right or left to avoid a large flat rock in the middle and the subsequent hydraulic. The New has narrowed to a width of some one hundred feet, and the water courses quickly through here.

The Class II+ Upper and Lower Kaymoor mark the river near mile twelve. Run to the right of center. Miller's Folly, a Class IV to IV+, then presents some danger elements. At the top of the rapid on the right side, beware an undercut rock where the current will try to force a raft. Attempt to run the first part of the rapid down the center. The second half of Miller's Folly flaunts a steep drop; veer to the right to miss the worst of the ensuing hole.

Whitewater fun at its best occurs on the Thurmond to Fayette Station part of the New River.

It was near here where Arnold, guide Brian Hager, and I once were a part of an epic duel with a trophy bronzeback. The sun was just beginning to slip behind the mountains that envelop West Virginia's New River Gorge when we pulled up to a series of car-sized boulders that dot the shoreline. As Hager manned the oars, Arnold and I began hurling buzzbaits to the little pockets of shade created by the huge rocks. Suddenly, Arnold reared back on his rod, and both Hager and I immediately realized that Dave had hooked an extraordinary smallmouth. Arnold shouted for Hager to keep the raft out of the main flow; a bronzeback of that size slashing through the heavy current of the gorge was not likely to be subdued. And Dave yelled for me to quickly grab a net. I need not have hurried. For the fish put on a classic and long-lasting smallmouth performance: three minutes of jumping, alternated with bottom hugging and line abrading, before the smallie finally came to the net. After a few quick photos and a measuring session, Arnold released the nineteen-inch smallmouth back into the New. That trophy bronzeback was just one of some thirty bass between twelve and nineteen inches that the three of us landed on a July float, a testament to how good the fishing can be.

The Thread the Needle area, a series of three boulders, is the next landmark. The current flows swiftly through this section. Then you will spot the Fayette Station Bridge, the Class IV Fayette Station Rapid (run this rollicking rapid down its center) and the New River Gorge Bridge. At 3,030 feet long, this bridge is the second longest single arch bridge in the world, and it also towers eight hundred and seventy-six feet above the river. What an appropriate way to end a three-state journey down the New River. On river left is the take-out—not only for this trip but for the river as a whole.

Soon downstream, the backwaters of Hawks Nest Lake begin to tame the New; and below Hawks Nest Lake Dam, the river is but a shadow of its former self. This section is called The Dries because of a four-mile-long tunnel that claims almost all of the river's water. Immigrants and indigent country people built this tunnel during the Great Depression. Because of horrendous working conditions and the desire to create the tunnel as quickly as possible for power generation purposes, hundreds of men are known to have died during, or because of, the construction process. Some 467 alone perished after contracting silicosis. So, for the purposes of this book, I end my coverage of the New at Fayette Station. One day, perhaps, the infamous tunnel can be closed and the New will run unencumbered until it unites with the Gauley River to form the Kanawha River. But that is another story for another time. Good luck and have fun on your personal exploration of the New River.

Appendices

APPENDIX A: Trip Planner
Guides, Canoe Liveries, and Outfitters

The New River in North Carolina and Virginia

Bluecat on the New
Donnie Turner
2800 Wysor Hwy.
Draper, VA 24324
(276) 776-3729
BlueCatsNewRiverOutfitters.com

Greasy Creek Outfitters
Darin R. Gillenwater
221 Marcom Drive NW
Riner, VA 24149
Cell: 540-230-6708
GreasyCreekOutfitters.com

Capt. Forest Pressnell
NewRiverCharter.com
info@NewRiverCharter.com
540-818-5274
facebook.com/pages/New-River-
Charter/118535391517225?ref=ts

New Angle Fishing Company
540-354-1774
facebook.com/NewAngleFishing-
Company/info

New River Fly Fishing (Mike Smith)
(540) 789-7811
NewRiverFlyfish.com
facebook.com/NewRiverFlyFishing

New River Canoe Rentals
3745 New River Parkway
Independence, VA 24348
(276) 773-3412 or 336-372-8793
CanoeingTheNew.com

New River Outdoor Company
Britt Stoudenmire
540-921-7438
NewRiverOutdoorCO.com

New River Outfitters
10725 US. Hwy 221 N.
P.O. Box 433
Jefferson, NC 28640
800-982-9190 or 336-982-9193
CanoeTheNew.com

RiverCamp USA
2221 Kings Creek Road,
Piney Creek, NC 28663
(336) 359-2267
RiverCampUSA.com

Riverside Canoe
2966 Garvey Bridge Rd.
Crumpler, NC 28617
336-982-9439
RiversideCanoeing.com

Rock On Charters (guides above and below Claytor)
540-588-6628 or 354-9424
RockOnCharters.net

Southern Musky Guide Service
SouthernMuskyGuideService.com
540-921-7438

Tangent Outfitters (Shawn Hash)
201 Cascade Drive
Pembroke, VA 24136
(540) 626-4567
NewRiverTrail.com

Zaloo's Canoes
3874 NC Highway 16 South
Jefferson, NC 28640
(800) 535-4027 or 336-246-3066
Zaloos.com

Tri-State Angler Guide Service
(Marty Shaffner)
(336) 957-4630 or (336) 902-0044
TriStateAngler.com

New River Below Bluestone Lake Dam

Outfitters in New River Gorge

ACE Adventure Resort
P.O. Box 1168
Oak Hill, WV 25901
800-787-3982
AceRaft.com

Adventures On The Gorge
P.O. Box 78
Lansing, WV 25862
855-633-2533
OnTheGorge.com

Cantrell Ultimate Rafting
49 Cantrell Dr.
Fayetteville, WV 25840
304-877-8235
CantrellUltimateRafting.com

New & Gauley River Adventures
P.O. Box 44
Lansing, WV 25862
800-759-7238
Gauley.com

River Expeditions
P. O. Box 9
Lansing, WV 25862
800-463-9873
RaftingInfo.com

West Virginia Outdoor Adventures
Tracy Asbury
1-888-PLAYWVA

WV River Adventures
231 Wood Mountain Road
Glen Jean, WV
800-292-0880
TryWVa.com

Fishing Guides

Fishing Companies in
the New River Gorge

Mountain Lake Bowfishing
304-575-8994

Mountain State Anglers
P. O. Box 78
Lansing, WV 25862
877-359-8463
MountainStateAnglers.com

New River Dories
P.O. Box 504
Mt. Hope, Â WV 25880
304-465-3332
NewRiverDories.com

Pro River Outfitters
P.O. Box 181
Lansing, WV 25862
304-575-5252
ProFishWV.com

Cindy Dragan
New River Gorge Bridge Day
OfficialBridgeDay.com
800-927-0263
304-640-8768 Cell

License and Fishing Regulations

North Carolina Wildlife Resources Commission
1701 Mail Service Center
Raleigh, NC 27699
(919) 707-0220
NCWildlife.org

Virginia Department of Game and Inland Fisheries
PO Box 111004
Richmond, VA 23230
(804) 367-1000
DGIF.Virginia.gov

West Virginia Division of Natural Resources
State Capitol, Bldg. 3
Charleston, WV 25305
(304) 348-2771
WVDNR.gov

Map Information

MapTech (topo maps). I use this company's maps extensively in the writing of this book.
877-587-9004 | MapTech.com

Two other useful publications that I use and can recommend are the *Virginia Atlas and Gazetteer* and the *West Virginia Atlas and Gazetteer*, available from:
DeLorme Mapping Company
PO Box 298
Freeport, ME 04032
(800) 227-1656 | Delorme.com

The best non-topo map I have found is *The New River Atlas*. It details the entire coverage area of this book. The contents of this book helped me immeasurably in writing this book and floating the river, and I strongly recommend New enthusiasts purchasing one. The guides also include much interesting information about the region's history, for more information: Vacanals.org

Land Protection: Conservation Easements

Blue Ridge Conservancy
BlueRidgeConservancy.org

DCR Office of Land Conservation
DCR.Virginia.gov/land_
conservation/index.shtml

Land Trust Alliance
LandTrustAlliance.org

New River Conservancy
NewRiverConservancy.org

New River Land Trust
NewRiverLandTrust.org

Valley Conservation Council
ValleyConservation.org

Virginia Outdoors Foundation
VirginiaOutdoorsFoundation.org

**VDACS Office of Farmland
Preservation**
VDACS.Virginia.gov/preservation

Tourism and Information Sources

North Carolina
**Alleghany Chamber of Commerce
and Visitors Center**
58 South Main Street
Sparta, NC 28675
(800) 372-5473
VisitAlleghanync.com/Virginia

West Virginia
Historic Fayetteville
(Fayette County)
P.O. Box 35
Fayetteville, WVÂ 25840
304-574-1500
888-574-1500
info@VisitFayettevilleWV.com
VisitFayettevillewv.com

New River Gateway CVB
(Summers County)
300 Second Avenue
Hinton, WVa 25951
304-466-5420
NewRiverGatewayCVB.com

New River Gorge (Fayette County)
310 Oyler Avenue
Oak Hill, WV 25901
800-927-0263
Sharon@NewRiverGorgeCVB.com
NewRiverGorgeCVB.com

Three Rivers Travel Council
206 Temple St.
Hinton, WVa 25951
304-466-5420
ThreeRiversWV.com

Southern West Virginia
(Raleigh, Summers, Mercer,
Fayette, Wyoming, McDowell,
Monroe Counties)
1406 Harper Road
Beckley, WVÂ 25801
304-252-2244
800-636-1460
VisitWV.com

Summersville (Nicholas County)
3 Armory Way
Summersville, WVÂ 26651
304-872-3722
866-716-0448
SummersvilleCVB.com

New River Gorge National River
National Park Service
PO Box 246
Glen Jean, WV 25846
(304) 465-0508
NPS.Gov/neri/home.htm
NPS.Gov/neri/index.htm

Lodging

Alleghany Inn
341 N Main St,
Sparta, NC 28675
888-372-2501 or 336 372-2501
AlleghanyInn.com

General Lewis Inn
301 East Washington Street
Lewisburg, WV 24901
(304) 645-4454 or (800) 628-4454
GeneralLewisInn.com
Glade Springs Resort
265 Resort Drive
Daniels, WV 25832
(800) 634-5233
GladeSprings.com

Visit Southern West Virginia
1408 Harper Road
Beckley, WV 25801
(800) VISIT-WV
VisitWV.com

West Virginia Department of Tourism
2101 Washington Street East
Charleston, WV 25305
(800) CALL-WVA
WVTourism.com

Helpful Web Sites

New River Gorge National River
NPS.Gov/neri/index.htm

National Weather Service:
erh.noaa.gov/marfc/james.shtml

USGS Current Water Data for Virginia
WaterData.usgs.gov/va/nwis/rt

North Carolina Real Time Streamflow Conditions
WaterData.usgs.gov/nc/nwis/current/?type=flow

Virginia Real Time Streamflow Conditions
WaterData.usgs.gov/va/nwis/rt

West Virginia Real Time Streamflow Conditions
Waterdata.usgs.gov/wv/nwis/rt

Appendix B: A Checklist of Birds Seen on the New between Spring and Fall

Note: I compiled this list with the aid of Mike Donahue, an avid birder and a member of the Virginia Society of Ornithology (VSO) from Roanoke, Virginia. As is true on any river, some of these birds dwell along the New year round and some are seasonal visitors appearing only in the early spring or late fall. The form and order of this list follows the VSO format. For more information on bird watching and the seasonal ranges of birds, consult field guides such as those published by Audubon and Peterson.

☐ Heron, Great Blue
☐ Heron, Green
☐ Egret, Great
☐ Heron Yellow-crowned
☐ Goose, Canada
☐ Mallard
☐ Duck, Wood
☐ Vulture, Turkey
☐ Hawk, Sharp-shinned
☐ Hawk, Cooper's
☐ Hawk, Red-tailed
☐ Hawk, Broad-winged
☐ Eagle, Bald
☐ Osprey
☐ Kestrel, American
☐ Grouse, Ruffed
☐ Bobwhite
☐ Turkey
☐ Killdeer
☐ Sandpiper, Spotted
☐ Dove, Rock

☐ Dove, Mourning
☐ Cuckoo, Yellow-billed
☐ Owl, Screech
☐ Owl, Great Horned
☐ Owl, Barred
☐ Chuck-Will's-Widow
☐ Whip-Poor-Will
☐ Nighthawk, Common
☐ Swift, Chimney
☐ Hummingbird, Ruby-throated
☐ Kingfisher, Belted
☐ Flicker, Common
☐ Woodpecker, Pileated
☐ Woodpecker, Red-bellied
☐ Woodpecker, Downy
☐ Flycatcher, Great Crested
☐ Phoebe, Eastern
☐ Flycatcher, Acadian
☐ Pewee, Eastern Wood
☐ Swallow, Tree
☐ Swallow, Bank

- ☐ Swallow, Rough-winged
- ☐ Swallow, Barn
- ☐ Jay, Blue
- ☐ Raven, Common
- ☐ Crow, Common
- ☐ Chickadee, Carolina
- ☐ Titmouse, Tufted
- ☐ Nuthatch, White-breasted
- ☐ Wren, House
- ☐ Wren, Carolina
- ☐ Mockingbird
- ☐ Catbird, Gray
- ☐ Thrasher, Brown
- ☐ Robin, American
- ☐ Thrush, Wood
- ☐ Thrush, Hermit
- ☐ Bluebird, Eastern
- ☐ Gnatcatcher, Blue-gray
- ☐ Kinglet, Golden-crowned
- ☐ Kinglet, Ruby-throated
- ☐ Waxwing, Cedar
- ☐ Starling
- ☐ Vireo, White-eyed
- ☐ Vireo, Yellow-throated
- ☐ Vireo, Solitary
- ☐ Vireo, Red-eyed
- ☐ Vireo, Warbling
- ☐ Warbler, Black-and-white
- ☐ Warbler, Worm-eating
- ☐ Warbler, Northern Parula

- ☐ Warbler, Yellow
- ☐ Warbler, Black-throated Green
- ☐ Warbler, Yellow-throated
- ☐ Warbler, Pine
- ☐ Warbler, Prairie
- ☐ Ovenbird
- ☐ Waterthrush, Louisiana
- ☐ Yellowthroat, Common
- ☐ Chat, Yellow-breasted
- ☐ Warbler, Hooded
- ☐ Redstart, American
- ☐ Meadowlark, Eastern
- ☐ Blackbird, Red-winged
- ☐ Oriole, Orchard
- ☐ Oriole, Baltimore
- ☐ Grackle, Common
- ☐ Cowbird, Brown-headed
- ☐ Tanager, Scarlet
- ☐ Cardinal
- ☐ Grosbeak, Rose-breasted
- ☐ Bunting, Indigo
- ☐ Goldfinch, American
- ☐ Towhee, Rufous-sided
- ☐ Bunting, Indigo
- ☐ Sparrow, Grasshopper
- ☐ Junco, Dark-eyed
- ☐ Sparrow, Chipping
- ☐ Sparrow, Field
- ☐ Sparrow, Song

Index

Fly and Spin Fishing for River Smallmouths (First E-Book Edition)

Fly and Spin Fishing for River Smallmouths is a motivating, informative guide for nature lovers of all kinds. The book delves into river bass fishing with easy-to-use tips on everything smallmouth, from lures and flies, types of cover to target, to strategies for cold and warm seasons, and much more. The book suggests enjoyable family-friendly river hobbies like canoeing, bird watching, river camping, and introducing children to the outdoors. This book also leads landowners, farmers, and adventurers in their efforts to protect our nation's waterways. From conservation easements to blueways, the author describes profitable and environmentally-enlightened government conservation programs.

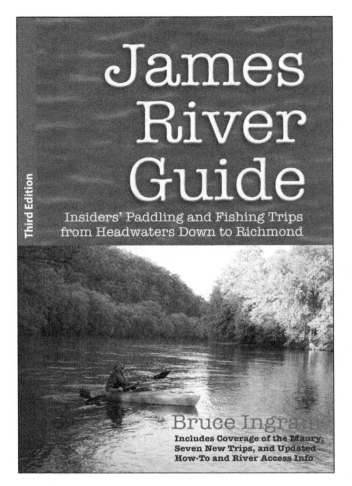

The James River Guide
(Third Edition)

The James River is Virginia's premier river for recreation—and the *James River Guide* is the key to enjoying it, whether you are an angler, kayaker, rafter or bird watcher. 29 locator maps provide vital information on the river, all the way from its headwaters near Iron Gate to the dramatic fall line at Richmond.

The longest river in the Old Dominion, the James offers some of the best smallmouth bass fishing in the state. Muskies and flathead catfish also abound, giving the recreational fisherman many exciting choices.

This new edition for 2015 includes updated and expanded information on favorite float trips, including new coverage of the marvelous Maury River, the main tributary of the Upper James; favorite fishing spots; updated access points; classic fishing lures; and directories of river guides and other resources.

About Secant Publishing

Featuring classics old and new, from an independent publisher based in the heart of Maryland's historic Eastern Shore. Our vision is to connect books of enduring interest with readers of discernment. See **SecantPublishing.com** for our growing list of titles.

About the Author

Bruce Ingram has spent a lifetime exploring the woods and waterways of his native Southwest Virginia. He is a devoted fisherman, birder, hunter, and paddler, sharing his love of the outdoors in five books and more than 2,000 magazine articles. A high school English teacher by day, Ingram lives with his wife Elaine in Troutville, Virginia. They have two children and two grandchildren.

The Outdoor Writers Association of America has honored Bruce six times for writing excellence. Follow Bruce's blog and keep up with his writing and speaking engagements at **https://sites.google.com/site/BruceIngramOutdoors/home** .

Made in the USA
Middletown, DE
03 August 2020

14396687R00126